Active History

American Revolution

Authors

Andi Stix, Ed.D., and PCC
Frank Hrbek, M.A.

SHELL EDUCATION

Contributing Authors

Wendy Conklin, M.S.

Stephanie Kuligowski, M.A.T.

Publishing Credits

Robin Erickson, *Production Director*; Lee Aucoin, *Creative Director*;
Timothy J. Bradley, *Illustration Manager*; Sara Johnson, M.S.Ed., *Editorial Director*;
Maribel Rendón, M.A.Ed., *Editor*; Kenya Wilkinson, M.A.T., *Editor;* Torrey Maloof, *Editor;*
Lexa Hoang, *Designer*; Grace Alba, *Designer;* Corinne Burton, M.A.Ed., *Publisher*

Image Credits

Cover, p.1 Library of Congress [LC-USZC4-4970]; p.35, 51, 58 The Granger Collection; p.84 United States National Park Service/Wikimedia; p.86 Luxrunner/Wikimedia; p.88 Center of Military History/Wikimedia; p.90 Benson John Lossing/Wikimedia; p.92 A Pictorial History of the United States, Goodrich, S. G. (1875)/Wikimedia; p.103 National Archives Experience/DOCS TEACH; p.113 Library of Congress [LC-DIG-ppmsca-07652]; p.115 Library of Congress [LC-DIG-hec-24344]; p.115 Library of Congress [LC-USZC4-5585]; all other images Shutterstock

Standards

© 2004 Mid-continent Research for Education and Learning (McREL)
© 2007 Teachers of English to Speakers of Other Languages, Inc. (TESOL)
© 2007 Board of Regents of the University of Wisconsin System. World-Class Instructional Design and Assessment (WIDA). For more information on using the WIDA ELP Standards, please visit the WIDA website at www.wida.us.
© 2010 National Council for the Social Studies (NCSS)
© 2010 National Governors Association Center for Best Practices and Council of Chief State School Officers (CCSS)

Shell Education

5301 Oceanus Drive
Huntington Beach, CA 92649-1030
http://www.shelleducation.com
ISBN 978-1-4258-1075-7
© 2014 Shell Educational Publishing, Inc.

Table of Contents

Research and Introduction

According to the position statement of the National Council for the Social Studies, "there is a profound difference between learning about the actions and conclusions of others, and reasoning one's way toward those conclusions. Active learning is not just 'hands-on,' it is 'minds-on'" (NCSS 2008).

The *Active History* series is designed to bring history to life in the classroom by providing meaningful experiences that allow students to learn the story behind the history. This book, *Active History: American Revolution*, brings your class face-to-face with the war in which America won its independence. It is true that even in the early years of the colonial experience, many other nations peopled America. But it is England that had the greatest impact. The United States is an English-speaking nation, and America's political, social, and economic institutions are the legacy of England's rule. The colonists may have chosen to go a different way, but when the break came, very little actually changed.

Understanding Active Learning

Active learning provides "engagement in learning; the development of conceptual knowledge and higher-order thinking skills; a love of learning; cognitive and linguistic development; and a sense of responsibility or 'empowerment' of students in their own learning" (Lathrop, Vincent, and Zehler 1993, 6). In essence, active learning inspires students to engage meaningfully in the content and take responsibility for their learning. It involves students as active participants in the learning process while incorporating higher-order thinking.

In the classroom, active learning can take on many forms. It often encompasses collaboration, various forms of grouping students through the learning process, independent-learning opportunities, and creative methods of output to demonstrate students' learning. An important feature in active-learning classrooms is that the students are the ones in the lead while the teacher acts as the coach. Some concrete examples are provided in the chart on the following page.

★★★

Research and Introduction *(cont.)*

Active Learning	
Example	**Nonexample**
Students are out of their seats, collaborating with peers on a project.	Students listen to a lecture.
Students use various forms of communication, like podcasting, to share their ideas with others.	Students quietly write responses to questions, using complete sentences.
Students use manipulatives to build models to demonstrate what they learned.	Students work written problems on a worksheet to show what they have learned.
Students create movie trailers to summarize a book they just read.	Students write a one-page book report.
Students participate in small-group discussions in efforts to produce ideas for solving a problem.	Students individually read research material and take notes.
Students use their bodies to act out a scene and demonstrate a newly learned concept.	Students give a two-sentence ticket-out-the-door reflection on what they learned.
Students are presented with higher-order questions that challenge their views and must consult other documents before answering.	Students answer lower-level questions over material they read to ensure basic comprehension.
Students work with primary-source documents to piece together details and clues about an event in history.	Students read a textbook to understand an event in history.

(Adapted from Conklin and Stix 2014)

Although many of the nonexamples make up pieces of typical classroom experiences and can support student learning when used appropriately and sparingly, they are not inherently active and will not produce the same depth and rigor of learning that the active learning practices do. Active learning produces more engaging opportunities for learning, and when students are more engaged, they spend more time investigating that content (Zmuda 2008).

Research and Introduction *(cont.)*

The simulations in *Active History: American Revolution* are grounded in making the students active participants in their own learning. They call for students to work in a variety of different groups to foster collaboration and communication and are designed to make students full participants who are good decision makers and competent problem solvers.

Active History: American Revolution also challenges students to develop speaking skills and the intellectual dexterity to debate and make speeches while being asked to take part in discussions, simulations, and/or debates. They learn to think systematically, to accept other viewpoints, and to tolerate and understand others. They are also encouraged to make their own investigations and to explore all areas of study to the fullest. In this way, they learn to rely on many inquiry methods to search and probe everywhere from the local library to the Internet. Students learn to rely on relevant documents, diaries, personal journals, photographs, newspaper articles, autobiographies, and contracts and treaties as well as period songs, art, and literature in order to support their active engagement and deep learning of the content.

Higher-Order Thinking Skills to Support Active Learning

A key component of active learning is the use of higher-order thinking skills. In order for students to be college- and career-ready, they need to be able to use these thinking skills successfully. Students use higher-order thinking when they encounter new or unfamiliar problems, questions, scenarios, or dilemmas (King, Goodson, and Rohani 1998). By structuring classroom practices that support students' use of higher-order thinking skills, you help them develop the necessary tools to be independent, creative, metacognitive, solution-driven individuals who can apply those skills outside the classroom.

Critical and creative thinking are the two key elements of higher-order thinking. Critical thinking entails one's careful analysis and judgment and "is self-guided, self-disciplined thinking which attempts to reason at the highest level of quality in a fair-minded way" (Scriven and Paul 1987). In support of this is creative thinking, which Heidi Hayes Jacobs (2010) suggests goes beyond reasonable and logical thinking. In fact, creativity is really a result of hard work and intentional thought, not luck or "magic" (Michalko 2006).

The simulations included in this book encourage students to think both critically and creatively to make decisions and solve problems. For example, students will work with primary-source materials, compose their own solutions and compare them to those that were actually made, and learn the celebrated and harsh realities of life during this period in history. Every part of *Active History* heightens the level of learning about a time in the past and helps students build their ability to apply their knowledge from language arts and other content areas to successfully complete each simulation.

Research and Introduction *(cont.)*

Using Simulations in the Active Classroom

A simulation is a teaching strategy that provides students with information based on an actual situation in time. It allows them to assume roles within the circumstances. By doing so, they analyze, make modifications to, and bring the event into current times. Students present differing points of view or solve the problem(s) involved in the situation. In looking at the qualities of an active-learning classroom, simulations are a great way to support students' independent learning, collaboration, communication, and active engagement in the social studies classroom.

Every simulation in this resource has students working together and going through group decision-making processes. Students are encouraged to use the Internet and other resources to support their learning. Brainstorming is a key function in many simulations. Initially, it generates concepts and ideas without judgment, speaking one's mind as well as listening to what others have to say, and, finally, narrowing the choices to fulfill the requirements of the lesson. Students voice their opinions and share their ideas as they go through the give-and-take of negotiating, compromising, and working out the final decision.

However, the learning process does not come to a stop at the conclusion of a particular simulation. Much of what students learn is useful information that can be transferred to a personal level. It is equally salient for students to see how the information affects their community and society. Therefore, the units often require students to seek out current information at the local level. Many of the lessons utilize opposing points of view. In the course of the lesson, speeches, dramatizations, debates, discussions, and written documents express these differing points of view. At the very least, the students come away with the understanding that there are at least two sides to every story. But more importantly, they also learn to be tolerant. If they speak well for their side on a particular issue, they must also listen well and have respect for the opposition. If any lesson in this unit instills in young minds tolerance, respect, civility, courtesy, understanding, and acceptance, we will have reached our goal.

Assessment

Assessment is a key part of instruction in any of today's classrooms. The results of assessments should be used to inform instruction and support students' future learning. It is important for students to understand how they will be assessed in order to truly allow them ownership over their learning. A collection of sample rubrics can be found on the Digital Resource CD and can be easily modified to meet the needs of students. To support student success in the classroom, negotiable contracting is crucial. Student input should be included when designing assessments.

Research and Introduction *(cont.)*

To support the implementation of negotiable contracting, follow these steps:

1. Ask students to imagine that they are the teacher and that they will be creating a list of criteria that should be used for assessing one another's ability to speak and behave properly during the simulation.

2. Have students work individually to create their own list.

3. Divide students into cooperative groups and allow them to share their ideas and consolidate their lists.

4. Call on a spokesperson from a group to submit one idea and record that idea on a sheet of chart paper.

5. Repeat this process, rotating from group to group. Once an idea is listed, it may not be restated again by another group. Allow students to use a checkmark on their lists for ideas shared by other groups. This skill is called *active listening*.

6. If the students have not thought of a certain criterion that you think is important and meaningful, add the item to the list and explain your reasoning to the class.

7. List the results on large chart paper as a reference guide and post it in a visible area of the classroom.

8. Negotiate with your students to agree on four or five of the criteria to use for assessment.

Sample suggestions for a class debate or discussion may be:

- Actively speaks and participates in discussion that demonstrates the understanding of the case
- Responds to another speaker who demonstrates comprehension of subject matter
- Asks quality questions that demonstrate logical thought
- Refers to his or her notes or any text with pertinent information
- Discusses the topic critically and tries to evaluate the topic from the particular time period

Research and Introduction *(cont.)*

Teacher as Coach

In the past, teachers have been defined as facilitators. But today, the new defined role of a teacher is one of a coach who offers inspiration, guidance, and training, and one who enhances students' abilities through motivation and support (Stix and Hrbek 2006).

The goal of a teacher coach is to increase student success by helping students:

- Find their inner strengths and passions in order to nurture self-worth and identity,
- Have a voice in their own learning and negotiate collectively with the instructor to create the goals and objectives,
- Passionately engage in discussion about content to increase memory retention and fuel motivation to learn,
- Use their inner talents to bring their work to the highest level of scholarship attainable.

The coaching strategies, which have been used successfully in some of the most diverse classrooms in the United States, can help to:

- Empower individuals by allowing them ownership of their work,
- Improve organizational and note-taking skills,
- Overcome emotional and environmental challenges,
- Resolve conflicts,
- Ensure harmonious group or team work.

The teacher as coach has the determined objective of having students find their own way within a given structure. The teacher coach encourages students to attain the learning skills needed to move on to a higher level of achievement while realizing their academic potential (Kise 2006). It allows students to work freely within a given structure so that they become more independent and authentically produce work as it relates to the content studied (Crane 2002). This philosophy parallels Charlotte Danielson's Framework, which many states are using as a basis for teacher evaluation (The Danielson Group 2013).

As an example, the teacher as coach can employ the GOPER Model. Instead of telling the students what to do, they follow this simple structure: What is your **g**oal? What are your **o**ptions? Design your **p**lan of operation? Discuss ahead of time, how you **e**liminate your obstacles. Now, **r**eflect on how well you accomplished your goal. For a sample coaching strategy called the GOPER Model, please refer to the Digital Resource CD.

How to Use This Book

The Structure of the Simulations

Active History: American Revolution includes five simulations. Although each simulation stands alone, when completed together in sequence, students gain a strong understanding of the American Revolution, its significance in American history, and how the concepts of the American Revolution are relevant to conflicts today.

The first four simulations present scenarios where students dig into the facts and circumstances of the American Revolution. The final simulation, Exercising Your Rights, brings the context of the American Revolution into more current times and has students identify a political conflict at the state or local level and debate the issue among the class.

The Role of Essential and Guiding Questions

Essential and guiding questions support the implementation of the simulations provided in this resource. The essential question is a defining one that serves as an umbrella for other guiding questions. It helps to link concepts and principles and frames opportunities for higher-level thinking. It is also so broad and open-ended that it cannot be answered in one sentence. To support the essential question, teachers should provide students with guiding questions. They relate to the big picture of the essential question but help narrow that question into its hierarchical components and often link subtopics together (Stix 2012).

In *Active History: American Revolution*, there is one essential question that guides students to synthesize their understanding as a result of participating in all of the simulations. Each simulation also includes up to four guiding questions to support the understanding of the essential question and probe students to think more deeply about the content.

How to Use This Book (cont.)

Objectives

The objectives provide a snapshot of the simulation and what students will be doing.

Standards and Materials

Each simulation targets one McREL social studies content standard and two Common Core anchor standards. A list of necessary materials is provided for quick reference and planning/preparation.

Questions

The overarching essential question and guiding questions are provided for easy reference throughout the lesson.

Pacing Guide

A suggested schedule is provided to support planning and preparation for the simulation. This plan is a suggestion and can be modified in other ways to best fit your instructional time blocks. The lessons are divided into days.

★★★

How to Use This Book *(cont.)*

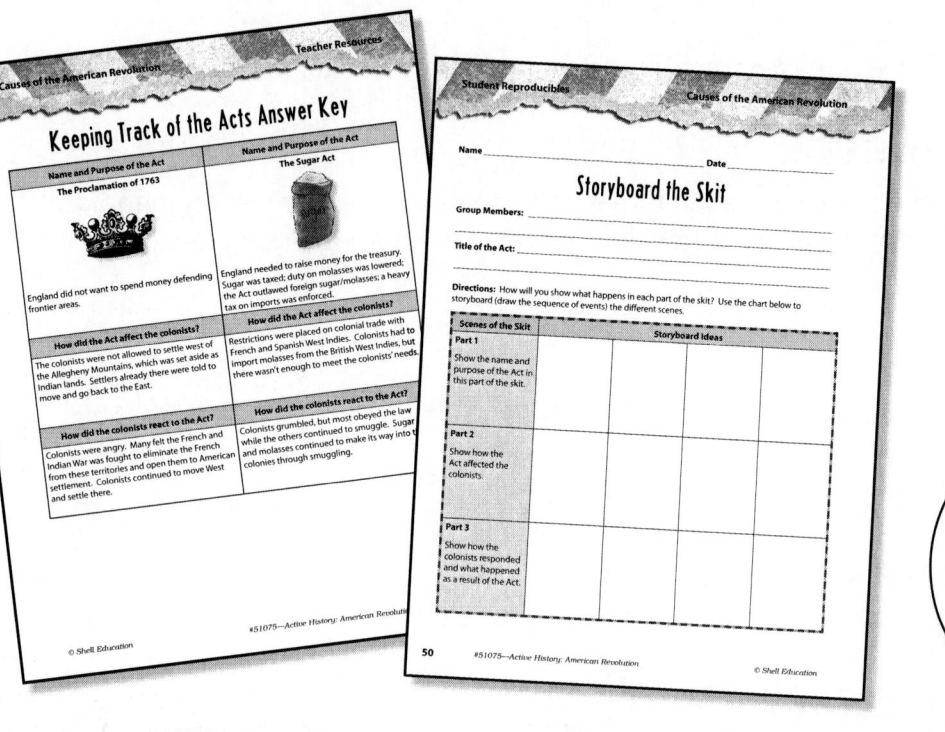

Teacher Resources

A step-by-step lesson plan is provided to guide teachers and students through the simulation. As a guide, the lesson plan is broken down into sections by suggested days. Any necessary teacher or student resources are referenced throughout the lesson plan.

Student Reproducibles

Any necessary student resources are provided at the end of each simulation lesson plan. These resources should be photocopied and provided to students throughout the course of the simulation. Resources include items such as planning guides, templates, rubrics, background-information pages, and graphic organizers.

Digital Resource CD

All necessary student and teacher resources are provided on the Digital Resource CD. A complete list of the contents of the Digital Resource CD can be found on pages 131–133.

Summaries of Simulations

1. Dramatizing the British Acts

In the first simulation, students read a copy of a British Act imposed on the colonies and conduct their own research to write and perform skits and roles dramatizing the impact of Parliament's tax laws. Students learn that governments sometimes make blunders that can push a people to open rebellion.

Acts Include:

- The Proclamation of 1763
- The Sugar Act, 1764
- Colonial Currency Act, 1764
- The Quartering Act, 1765
- The Stamp Act, 1765
- The Declaratory Act, 1766
- The Townshend Acts, 1767
- The Tea Act, 1773
- The Quebec Act, 1774
- The Intolerable Acts, 1774

2. Making Mystery Boxes

In the second simulation, students create a Mystery Box about an outstanding individual who lived during the War for Independence and the period immediately following when the United States of America came into existence. Students use the inquiry approach to obtain biographical information about those people who were associated with these important historical events.

Historical Figures Include:

Samuel Adams	Betsy Ross	Charles Wilson Peale	George Rogers Clark
George Washington	Benedict Arnold	Marquis de Lafayette	Henry Knox
Benjamin Franklin	George Grenville	Baron von Steuben	Major John Pitcairn
Paul Revere	Mercy Otis Warren	Nathan Hale	Daniel Shays
Patrick Henry	Crispus Attucks	John Stark	James Madison
Thomas Jefferson	Alexander Hamilton	Mary Ludwig Hays	Edmund Randolph
King George III	John Paul Jones	Charles Cornwallis	General John Burgoyne
Henry Lee	Horatio Gates	Phillis Wheatley	Aaron Burr
Deborah Sampson	John Adams	Francis Marion	Thaddeus Kosciuszko
General William Howe	Ethan Allen	Abigail Smith Adams	General Thomas Gage
Thomas Paine	John Hancock	James Wilkinson	Chief Joseph Brant

★★★

Summaries of Simulations (cont.)

3. Building Battlefield Tours

In the third simulation, students design a travel guide for tourists. The guides provide information identifying the route to take with accompanying maps. They describe special sights, give historical background, provide pictures, offer details on what the climate was like, and characterize the natural surroundings. An audio recording provides further details about the battles.

Battles include:

- Lexington and Concord
- New York Campaign
- Battle of Trenton
- Battle of Saratoga
- Battle of Yorktown

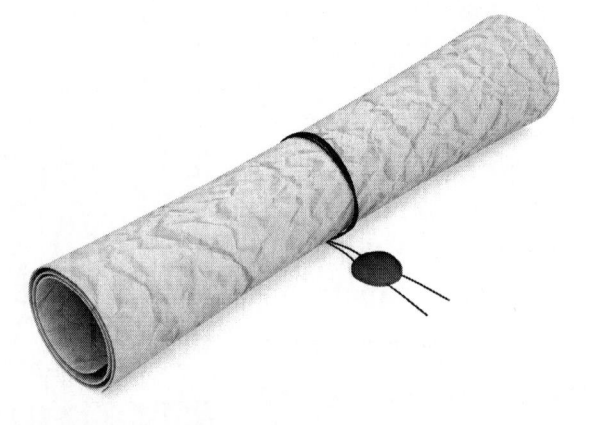

4. Forming a New Government

In the fourth simulation, students undertake the task of creating a government in which the states retain their powers at the expense of the central government. Students use Jefferson's indictment of King George III in the Declaration of Independence as their starting point for creating their own version of the new government taking power after the War of Independence. Each group writes its own portion of the Articles of Confederation, based upon the grievances they have been assigned to rectify. The class creates booklets for a new government. The students' Articles of Confederation may be supplemented with diagrams, charts, and pictures.

5. Exercising Your Rights

In this final simulation, students exercise their democratic rights and responsibilities to actively participate in government by identifying a political conflict at the state or local level. They research the issues involved in the conflict and examine the viewpoints on those issues. Students then form an opinion, take a stance, and engage in public debate about the issues.

Correlations to Standards

Shell Education is committed to producing educational materials that are research and standards based. In this effort, we have correlated all our products to the academic standards of all 50 United States, the District of Columbia, the Department of Defense Dependent Schools, and all Canadian provinces.

How to Find Standards Correlations

To print a customized correlations report of this product for your state, visit our website at **http://www.shelleducation.com** and follow the on-screen directions. If you require assistance in printing correlations reports, please contact Customer Service at 1-800-858-7339.

Purpose and Intent of Standards

Legislation mandates that all states adopt academic standards that identify the skills students will learn in kindergarten through grade twelve. Many states also have standards for pre-K. This same legislation sets requirements to ensure the standards are detailed and comprehensive.

Standards are designed to focus instruction and guide adoption of curricula. Standards are statements that describe the criteria necessary for students to meet specific academic goals. They define the knowledge, skills, and content students should acquire at each level. Standards are also used to develop standardized tests to evaluate students' academic progress.

Teachers are required to demonstrate how their lessons meet state standards. State standards are used in the development of all our products, so educators can be assured they meet the academic requirements of each state.

McREL Compendium

We use the Mid-continent Research for Education and Learning (McREL) Compendium to create standards correlations. Each year, McREL analyzes state standards and revises the compendium. By following this procedure, McREL is able to produce a general compilation of national standards. Each lesson in this product is based on one or more McREL standards. The chart on the following pages lists each standard taught in this product and the page numbers for the corresponding lessons.

TESOL Standards

The lessons in this book promote English language development for English language learners. The standards listed on the following pages support the language objectives presented throughout the lessons.

Common Core State Standards

The texts in this book are aligned to the Common Core State Standards (CCSS). The standards correlation can be found on pages 16–17.

Correlations to Standards (cont.)

Correlation to Common Core State Standards

The lessons in this book are aligned to the Common Core State Standards (CCSS). Students who meet these standards develop the skills in reading that are the foundation for any creative and purposeful expression in language.

Grade(s)	Standard	Page(s)
K–12	**R.3** Analyze how and why individuals, events, or ideas develop and interact over the course of a text.	62–65
K–12	**R.7** Integrate and evaluate content presented in diverse formats and media, including visually and quantatively, as well as in words.	77–81
K–12	**R.8** Delineate and evaluate the argument and specific claims in a text, including the validity of the reasoning as well as the relevance and sufficiency of the evidence.	103–105
K–12	**R.10** Read and comprehend complex literary and informational texts independently and proficiently.	21–23 113–117
K–12	**W.2** Write informative/explanatory texts to examine and convey complex ideas and information clearly and accurately through the effective selection, organization, and analysis of content.	103–105
K–12	**W.8** Gather relevant information from multiple print and digital sources, assess the credibility and accuracy of each source, and integrate the information while avoiding plagiarism.	113–117
K–12	**W.9** Produce clear and coherent writing in which the development, organization, and style are appropriate to task, purpose, and audience.	62–65
K–12	**SL.2** Integrate and evaluate information presented in diverse media and formats, including visually, quantitatively, and orally.	21–23
K–12	**SL.4** Present information, findings, and supporting evidence so that listeners can follow the line of reasoning and the organization, development, and style are appropriate to task, purpose, and audience.	77–81

★★★

Correlations to Standards *(cont.)*

Correlation to McREL Standards

Content	Standard	Page(s)
United States History	**6.2** Students will understand the events that contributed to the outbreak of the American Revolution and the earliest armed conflict of the Revolutionary War.	21–23
United States History	**6.4** Students will understand the major developments and chronology of the Revolutionary War and the roles of its political, military, and diplomatic leaders.	77–81
United States History	**6.5** Students will understand the perspectives of and the roles played in the American Revolution by various groups of people.	62–65
United States History	**8.1** Students will understand events that led to and shaped the Constitutional Convention.	103–105
Civics	**28.1** Students will understand how participation in civic and political life can help citizens attain individual and public goals.	113–117

★★★

Background Information for the Teacher

That the American colonies would eventually rebel was considered inevitable on both sides of the Atlantic Ocean. The issue may not have been openly addressed in any public forum, but utterances along those lines ricocheted in the corridors of power in both England and the colonies. The settlements in America had grown rapidly and prospered, as had England's wealth and power in direct proportion to the trade that emanated from America. Mercantilistic policies guaranteed England a favorable balance of trade with her colonies, and it was a trade that increased with every passing year, making London merchants and traders happy with their prosperity. America's raw materials flowed in a steady stream across the Atlantic Ocean and up the Thames River, where wharves and docks continually stocked the fuel that kept England's shopkeepers and manufacturers busy and fully occupied.

The American colonists also benefited from their trade with the mother country but not to the extent enjoyed by their British counterparts. England's exports were greater than its imports every year, as laws had been enacted over the years restricting the colonies from developing their own industries and manufacturers. In this manner, mercantilism gave England an advantage over its colonial possessions, the prevailing attitude being that the colonies existed for the prosperity and well-being of the mother country.

It was the Seven Years War in Europe (1755–1763), called The French and Indian War in America, that brought many of the issues that existed between England and her colonies out into the open. Many Englishmen and American colonists were aware that England's trade with America had increased dramatically in the eighteenth century (1700s). As America's trade with Europe declined, it became apparent that America was not dependent on her trade with England to the extent that Englishmen had become dependent on American goods and raw materials.

England needed her colonies more than they needed her. The balance of trade continued to favor the British, but the Americans were also getting benefits that were more important than mere monetary considerations. The American trade was vital to British interests and her prosperous economy. If the trade was jeopardized, it was in England's interest to protect the colonies. American colonists knew they enjoyed the protection from external enemies that only the Royal Navy could provide.

From the middle of the seventeenth century and on into the 1700s, England and France had been involved in a series of wars in Europe. France was the dominant power on the European continent, and England's policy was to contain the growing dominance of France through a series of alliances with the other kingdoms of Europe. The issue of trade and commerce was another reason for the series of wars, with both England and France anxious to establish their power in the West Indies, in India, on the coast of Africa, and throughout Asia. America, too, became a battleground. Along the St. Lawrence River, the French established two important settlements at Quebec and Montreal back in the early years of the seventeenth century.

Background Information for the Teacher *(cont.)*

Over the years, the French looked at their settlements in New France more as a business rather than as colonies they could exploit by encouraging widespread immigration. Frenchmen spread out in all directions, exploring the Great Lakes and the Ohio River Valley and winding their way down the Mississippi River to the Gulf of Mexico and into Texas. It became apparent that the French surrounded England's settlements along the Atlantic seaboard.

Expansion westward and beyond the Alleghenies was blocked. It was the French presence to the north and west that was a threat to the English colonists. In the first three wars with France—called King William's War, Queen Anne's War, and King George's War here in America—the colonists raised militias for their own defense and grudgingly assisted British regular troops on occasion. It was the Royal Navy and England's dominance at sea that gave colonists the greatest feeling of security. As England became dependent on the colonies for trade, the colonies depended on England for protection against the French.

All of this came to a sudden end with the signing of the Treaty of Paris in 1763, which ended the Seven Years War. By 1759, the fighting had ended in America, with British armies victorious in every campaign and occupying both Montreal and Quebec. France had gone down in defeat, and certain territories that the French possessed were relinquished to the conqueror. England's ministers and leaders had to decide whether they would take Guadeloupe or Canada; France would surrender one but not both and was willing to make this concession to end the disastrous war. Guadeloupe was a sugar island and would add immensely to England's growing empire in terms of wealth and power, but Canada, too, was a tempting choice. Adding their voices to the growing debate were those individuals who warned that the Americans might break away. If England took Canada, the American colonists would no longer be dependent on the British and the Royal Navy for protection from an external enemy.

Further indicating America's potential desire for independence was its steady increase in population. Doubling every 25 years, the population of the thirteen colonies was close to 2.5 million people by the end of the Seven Years War.

The colonists were rich and prosperous; even America's poor weren't so badly off. Cities like New York, Boston, Philadelphia, and Charleston were equal to any great city in England, except London. Visitors from England and Europe always remarked that beggars were nowhere in evidence. Hard work was never an issue for the Americans, for they relished the opportunity to make a better life for themselves and their children. Many Englishmen saw that if the population continued to grow as it did, and if America's wealth and prosperity increased, the colonists would be able to determine for themselves that they no longer had to depend on the English. When England took New France as a prize of war in 1763, the American colonists were suddenly freed of a threatening enemy and of their dependence on England for protection from an external enemy. England's worst fears about its American possessions were soon to become a reality.

Background Information for the Teacher (cont.)

Despite England's awarenesss of the colonies' rapid development, their heavy involvement in the European conflicts led to very loose governance of American possessions. Over time, each of the thirteen colonies had its own legislative assembly, and each jealously guarded the right and privilege to tax itself. England appointed royal governors, but they were paid by colonial legislatures, ensuring that the officials coming to America from England would be malleable and cooperative. Americans wanted the royal governors to be responsive to their needs and to work cooperatively with them. Letters from royal governers are filled with whining and complaining about their treatment at the hands of the colonists, who refused to pay salaries and only grudgingly cooperated with the royal appointees who sought to impose the king's will and directives.

The colonists took every opportunity they could seize to thwart and forestall royal authority. The Navigation Acts were on the books, but the laws were largely ignored. The ships and sloops of the colonists sailed to all parts of the world into which they desired to venture, and they traded and exchanged goods wherever they had the chance. Smuggling goods became an active livelihood, and the colonists carried it on with a passion whenever the opportunity arose. England was 3,000 miles away, and this great distance was an impediment to exerting efficient control over colonial activities. It was particularly galling to the British, while fighting the series of wars with France for their very survival, to find that the colonists were carrying on trade with the French West Indies for sugar and molasses. Even though William Pitt and the ministers in his cabinet sought to end this trade through orders to the governors and the Royal Navy, it was to no avail. The Americans needed the molasses and the sugar for the rum distilleries in the New England settlements, and the sugar islands that were in British hands simply could not supply what the colonists needed.

Though the American colonists were largely dependent on England for protection against the French in the Canadian settlements, once that threat was removed, it spelled a change in the relationship with their British "cousins." In all other spheres, the colonists were able to go their own way. When the king, his ministers, and Parliament sought to redefine the relationship with the American colonies by imposing new laws and some semblance of order, everything unraveled. The new policy came into being with the Proclamation of 1763, a direct response to Pontiac's War which was the largest Indian uprising experienced by the British in all its years in America. The lands west of the Alleghenies were to be closed to settlement and would be Indian Territory, closely administered by royal authorities.

Trade with the Indians would be closely controlled, troops would be stationed at outposts, and land speculation by colonists would be curtailed. Money would be needed to pay for troops along the frontier, and the colonists were taxed accordingly by Parliament to defray these military expenses. It was the dozen years prior to Lexington and Concord that would drive the angered, heavily taxed American colonists into open rebellion and would make a reality of the fears that Englishmen had always had in the backs of their minds.

Dramatizing the British Acts

Objectives

- Students will discover that unpopular decisions made by governments can cause people to rebel.
- Students will write skits that present and explain the British Acts imposed on the colonists.

Standards

- McREL United States History Level II, 6.2
- CCSS.ELA-Literacy.CCRA.R.10
- CCSS.ELA-Literacy.CCRA.SL.2

Materials List

- Reproducibles (pages 24–54)
- Teacher Resources (pages 55–61)
- Index cards
- Large chart paper

Overarching Essential Question

What is independence?

Guiding Questions

- For what reasons did the British feel justified in imposing taxes on the American colonists?
- In what ways did the Americans respond to the British Acts?
- Evaluate and explain the most intolerable act.
- Describe in detail the effect that the taxes had on the Americans.

Suggested Schedule

The schedule below is based on a 45-minute period. If your school has block scheduling, please modify the schedule to meet your own needs.

Day 1	Day 2	Day 3	Day 4	Day 5
Introductory Vocabulary Activity Students **study assigned Acts** and **brainstorm skits**.	Students **write skits** in assigned groups.	Students **practice skits** in assigned groups.	Students **perform skits** in assigned groups.	Students **finish skit performances, reflect, and assess**.

Dramatizing the British Acts *(cont.)*

Introductory Activity

1. Divide the class into seven groups. Distribute copies of the *Student Glossary* (pages 24–27) to students. Divide up the glossary words and give each group three different words. Ask each group to write definitions for their assigned glossary words on large sheets of chart paper, so the group can view it.

2. Students can check their definitions and understandings of the words with the *Student Glossary Answer Key* provided on pages 55–56.

3. Have groups write 2–4 rap lines to demonstrate their understanding of the glossary words they were assigned. The groups' raps should use the word in context and/or define the words in a clever way. Have the groups perform their raps for the class. After each performance, the rest of students should fill in their *Student Glossary* sheet (pages 24–27) for the words presented. This way, all students will become familiar with all of the words and be prepared for the skits. You can also place each vocabulary word on an index card and post them in the classroom for a word wall. As an option, they can be hung using hook-and-loop fasteners so that they can be charted in different ways.

Day 1

1. Divide students into 10 groups. Assign a different act to each group. You may decide to modify the amount of groups based on the number of students in your class.

2. Distribute the corresponding summary pages that describe the British Acts imposed on the colonies (pages 28–47) to each group. Students should read both sheets independently. The first sheet lists just the facts. The second sheet tells what really happened. Ask students to highlight the essential parts of the story with a highlighter and discuss them with their groups. (Point out that they will see many of the vocabulary words they already reviewed in these pages.)

3. Explain to students that they will create original skits to act out for the class. Distribute copies of the *Skit Planning Sheet* (page 48) to students. Have each group work together to complete their sheets using information from their Acts. This will serve as a guide for their skits.

4. Distribute one copy of the *Set the Scene* sheet (page 49) to each group and model this activity. On this sheet, students will list the characters included in their skits, describe the setting, and define the plot. The description of the setting will be read aloud prior to the performance of the skit. Encourage students to be as detailed as possible in their setting descriptions.

5. Distribute a copy of the *Storyboard the Skit* sheet (page 50) to each group and model for the class. Students will use this page to further define the scenes in their skits. Tell students to keep their skits under five minutes. Engage in negotiable contracting of assessment with the students.

Dramatizing the British Acts (cont.)

Days 2–3

1. Once the groups have finished planning for their skits using the sheets from the previous day, discuss as a class the expectations for students' skits. Remind groups that the skit must incorporate the content listed on the *Skit Planning Sheet* (page 48) and should not exceed five minutes in length.

2. Have groups begin to write their scripts. Groups may prefer to write their scripts on computers, if available. If groups handwrite their scripts, be prepared to make copies of the final scripts for each group member to reference during the performance.

3. If time permits, you may want to pair groups and have them peer edit each other's scripts. Inform students that they may bring in or make props if they so desire.

4. The final step in their preparations is to practice the skit. Students should refer to the rubric on the *Skit Assessment* form (page 54), as a guide and practice.

Day 4

1. Have the groups perform their skits.

2. While each group performs their skit, the rest of the class will use copies of the *Keeping Track of the Acts* sheet (pages 51–53) to take notes about each of the Acts. An answer key is provided on the *Keeping Track of the Acts Answer Key* sheet (pages 57–61).

3. Assess student skits using the *Skit Assessment* sheet (page 54).

Day 5

1. After the skits have been performed, have students look over their notes written on the *Keeping Track of the Acts* sheet (pages 51–53).

2. Place students into small groups and have each group discuss the overarching essential question as it relates to what they have just learned: *What is independence?*

3. Present the guiding question to students: *For what reasons did the British feel justified in imposing taxes on the American colonists?* Have students write 1–2 paragraphs explaining their answers as a reflection and an assessment of what they learned.

4. After a few minutes of discussion, allow groups to present their final answer aloud for the entire class.

Name _____ Date _____

Student Glossary

Directions: You have been assigned a few of these words. Find their meanings and plan how you will use the words in your rap. After other raps are performed, write the definitions for the remaining words. Keep this glossary and use it to help you as you work through the unit.

1. **abstain (v)**

   definition: _____

   How it is used in the rap: _____

2. **boycott (v, n)**

   definition: _____

   How it is used in the rap: _____

3. **Conservative (n)**

   definition: _____

   How it is used in the rap: _____

4. **defy (v)/defiance (n)**

   definition: _____

   How it is used in the rap: _____

5. **delegate (n)/delegation (n)**

   definition: _____

   How it is used in the rap: _____

Student Glossary *(cont.)*

6. **distiller (n)**

   definition: _____

   How it is used in the rap: _____

7. **duty (trade) (n)**

   definition: _____

   How it is used in the rap: _____

8. **grievance (n)**

   definition: _____

   How it is used in the rap: _____

9. **Loyalist (n)**

   definition: _____

   How it is used in the rap: _____

10. **mercantilism (n)**

    definition: _____

    How it is used in the rap: _____

11. **mercenary (n)**

    definition: _____

    How it is used in the rap: _____

Student Glossary *(cont.)*

12. militia (n)

definition: _____

How it is used in the rap: _____

13. Minutemen (n)

definition: _____

How it is used in the rap: _____

14. Moderate (n)

definition: _____

How it is used in the rap: _____

15. Patriot (n)

definition: _____

How it is used in the rap: _____

16. petition (n)

definition: _____

How it is used in the rap: _____

17. quartering (v)

definition: _____

How it is used in the rap: _____

Student Glossary *(cont.)*

18. Radical (n)

definition: _____

How it is used in the rap: _____

19. resolution (n)

definition: _____

How it is used in the rap: _____

20. servitude (n)

definition: _____

How it is used in the rap: _____

21. treason (n)

definition: _____

How it is used in the rap: _____

22. unanimous (adj)

definition: _____

How it is used in the rap: _____

The Proclamation of 1763
Just the Facts

Date: 1763

Provisions of the Law

- It temporarily outlawed settlements west of the Allegheny Mountains.
- The rich Indian trade was placed under royal license.
- All land purchases from the western Indians were cancelled.
- Frontiersmen living in the Ohio River Valley were required to leave the area.

Reasons for the British Action

- Britain's triumph in the French and Indian War (1754–1763)
- Britain's need to defend vast territories
- Pontiac's uprising in 1763
- Britain's war debt in excess of 120 million pounds

How the Proclamation Was Enforced

It could not be enforced. The western flow of settlers could not be stopped. The Proclamation of 1763 was like an open sore that just wouldn't heal. It continued to be a major colonial complaint against King George up until the Revolution.

Points of View

Patriots/Radicals: This group ignored the Proclamation of 1763 and continued to migrate into the Ohio River Valley (Ohio, Kentucky, Tennessee). Most of the colonists ignored it, too. This law could not be enforced. The British would have had to arm the border with more than 100,000 soldiers along the entire frontier region, from Maine down to Georgia.

Loyalists: Many of the "Conservatives" were land buyers and made fortunes on land purchases in the Ohio River Valley. They were against any measure that made it hard for them to make money or cut into their profits. For these reasons, they were against the Proclamation of 1763.

Moderates: Any in this group wanting to move west into the Ohio River Valley were opposed to the Proclamation of 1763. If they were interested in buying land, they were against it. Many probably had no opinion one way or the other.

The Proclamation of 1763
What Really Happened?

At the end of the French and Indian War (1754–1763), England had defeated all of its enemies. The British army had victories in Europe, North America, India, the West Indies, and Southeast Asia. With the signing of the Treaty of Paris in 1763, France's influence was completely eliminated from North America. Canada and all of the lands east of the Mississippi River to the Atlantic Ocean now belonged to England. Great Britain was supreme. But it was also hated and envied by the other nations of Europe. Many of these enemies were just waiting for the chance to get revenge for past humiliations. The vast territories gained after years of struggle now had to be protected. A great Indian uprising in 1763 led by Chief Pontiac was a clear warning of how weak the border was with the absence of British soldiers.

England had a war debt of 120 million pounds sterling (the British currency). The mother country wanted to keep the expense of the empire, especially the maintenance of the troops along the frontier and in the outposts, at a minimum. The king and his ministers had a ready solution, and it was clearly stated in the Proclamation of 1763. No settlers would be allowed west of the Allegheny Mountains. This would ensure that the Native Americans would remain at peace. Large groups of peaceful British soldiers would not have to be housed in the western regions to keep the peace and protect settlers if the American Indians remained. The land west of the Alleghenies would be Indian hunting grounds. Anyone settled in that region would have to move and resettle in the east.

The colonists were angered by the Proclamation of 1763. As far as they were concerned, this was a poor attempt to hold back the westward movement. Most colonists simply ignored the Proclamation of 1763 and continued to move across the mountains into the Ohio River Valley. The colonists wanted the lands west of the Alleghenies regardless of the proclamation in place. After all, why else was the French and Indian War fought? The reaction to the Proclamation of 1763 was the first of the complaints the colonists raised against the British government, and it remained a source of resentment to the War for Independence in 1775.

The Sugar Act
Just the Facts

Date: 1764

Provisions of the Law

- It created a new tax placed on sugar and syrup and enforced the old Navigation Acts and Molasses Act.
- It raised the duty on refined sugar.
- It outlawed foreign rum.
- It lowered duties on foreign molasses.
- It placed a heavy tax on foreign imports (unless shipped through England).

Reasons for the British Action

- To lower the war debt
- To bring more money into the treasury
- To make colonists pay their share of the annual British cost for keeping order throughout the colonies
- To make money from the colonies through trade
- To make sure the colonies obeyed the laws

How the Sugar Act Was Enforced

The colonists complained but obeyed the law. There were no major outbursts of violence. Of course, the colonists were always creative in avoiding what they considered "unnecessary duties." They continued to smuggle whatever they needed. The Royal Navy was assigned as custom agents and coast guards to check incoming and outgoing shipments, but the colonists usually managed to outwit them.

Points of View

Patriots/Radicals: From this group, there was a bit of complaining but no real action or disobedience. The honest merchants continued to maintain their honesty, were obedient to the crown, and obeyed the law.

Loyalists: The conservative group, especially merchants and distillers who were directly affected by the law, were the ones who grumbled the loudest. Here were the beginnings of an uneasy partnership between Radicals (Patriots) and Conservatives (Loyalists), as they had mutual interests. They both felt that the taxation by England's Parliament was unjust, as it clearly dipped into the pockets of the upper-class merchants, businessmen, distillers, and bankers.

Moderates: They were not terribly affected by the Sugar Act and remained a watch-and-wait audience to the events that were unfolding.

The Sugar Act
What Really Happened

The Sugar Act produced some desired revenue for England, but it also caused an equal amount of colonial complaints and anger. The Grenville Ministry, in its eagerness to raise money, tried to enforce the old Acts of Trade and Navigation. These were the foundations of England's great empire and its policy of mercantilism. By controlling trade and making the balance of trade favorable to the mother country, England brought wealth and prosperity to its merchants and businessmen. The thirteen colonies could only trade with England. If foreign trade existed with Europe or any other part of the world, goods first had to be shipped to England, where import taxes were paid, and then they could be sent on to North America. Additionally, trade goods could be carried only on English ships. Restrictions were placed on what the colonies could manufacture, making them wholly dependent on the developing industries of England. Many colonial products and resources could only be traded with England.

The Molasses Act was a part of this mercantile policy. Molasses was used in the manufacturing of rum and was vital to the distillers of New England. The French, Spanish, and British all harvested sugar from the West Indies. The Molasses Act forced the colonists to buy only from the British planters in the West Indies, whose supply was inadequate for what the distillers needed. The king's response to the colonists was that they should buy from the British or stop making rum. The colonists protested. When their complaints were ignored, they ignored the law and began smuggling the goods they needed to make a profit.

Little effort had been made to enforce the Molasses Act. At the time, England was involved in European wars and building other colonies in foreign lands. The smuggling was common, and enforcement remained nonexistent. George Grenville, the British Prime Minister, recognized all the potential revenue that had been lost over a span of decades. He replaced the Molasses Act with the Sugar Act. He also called for the customs laws to be strictly enforced and the trade duties collected. The new Act lowered the duty on molasses but raised the duty on sugar. The British made a strong effort to enforce the Sugar Act. The colonists complained bitterly with outrage, and the smuggling was carried on with a business-as-usual attitude. Eventually, during the 1763–1775 period as unrest began to sweep across the colonial landscape, the duties imposed by the Sugar Act were lowered.

The Colonial Currency Act
Just the Facts

Date: 1764

Provisions of the Law

- It outlawed further printing of paper money because too much was being manufactured, which lowered its value.
- It prevented colonial debtors from settling their accounts in old, cheap currency.

Effects of the Law

- All duties and losses were to be paid in coined money, gold, or silver
- Enforcement of the Old Trade Acts
- Cut off the profitable West Indies trade

★★★

How the Colonial Currency Act Was Enforced

The Royal Navy operated as a coast guard and customs police force, but the colonists continued to smuggle. In many parts of the colonies, smuggling was considered a respectable profession and a means of earning a decent living—just like piracy. The governors and many of the king's men shared in the abundant profits of smuggling and piracy. The colonists protested, but many still continued to smuggle goods. Enforcement of the trade laws became strict, so smuggling was simply carried on with a greater degree of stealth.

Points of View

Patriots/Radicals: They were horrified by the law, which disrupted the colonial economy. Cheap paper money issued by the colonial governments was declared illegal. Also, since the Sugar Act outlawed trade with the French and Spanish West Indies, they were furious that their major sources of gold and silver coins were inaccessible to them. So the colonists continued the illegal trade with the French and Spanish to ensure their access to the new currency. Through this illegal trade, gold and silver coins entered the colonial economy.

Loyalists: Many of the conservative groups (merchants, bankers, businessmen) became partners with the Radicals. The Colonial Currency Act was bad for the economy and bad for business.

Moderates: Most (if they were farmers) were not affected. They bartered for what they needed. They had no real opportunity to get their hands on gold or silver. They favored cheap money, and here they probably had opinions in common with the Radicals.

The Colonial Currency Act
What Really Happened?

Prime Minister George Grenville may have been brilliant in working with figures and numbers, but as a judge of human nature, he was a dud. Either he simply did not understand the Americans, or he thought that Americans were "cowardly," "base," "worthless," "lazy," "ingrates," "unworthy of England's generosity," "scoundrels," and "wretches." The English upper classes were convinced that these were the traits common to all Americans. Grenville imagined that Americans were followers, like sheep, and in a sheep-like manner would accept his financial laws.

The Sugar Act called for duties and losses to be paid in gold and silver coins. However, since the trade with the French and Spanish West Indies was prohibited, the flow of gold and silver coins was cut off. Under the Colonial Currency Act, no more paper money could be issued by the colonies. It was little wonder that the colonial economy was in trouble or that the colonists imagined the British were determined to destroy it. Colonists repeatedly complained of "bankruptcies," "lack of gold and silver," "unfavorable balance of trade," and "unjust taxation."

The Colonial Currency Act simply fanned the flames of a fire that was already on the brink of burning beyond control. The colonists continued to trade with the French and the Spanish. Gold and silver coins jingled in their pockets. Many hearty souls were unfortunate and struggled to survive. Others, who were less fortunate, suffered from these laws and ended up joining the ranks of the Radicals to resist the king and Parliament.

The Quartering Act
Just the Facts

Date: 1765

Provisions of the Law

- If barracks were not available, colonial homes would be used to house soldiers.
- The colonists would furnish the troops with fuel, candles, vinegar, salt, bedding, cooking utensils, and a minimal amount of beer, cider, and rum.
- The colonists were to be reimbursed (have their money paid back) by the colonial government, and the rates were to be fixed by the Act.

Reasons for the British Action

- To cut down the expenses of protecting Britain's American territories.
- To have the colonies pay part of the bill for the expense of being protected by the king's navy and king's troops.

How the Quartering Act Was Enforced

It was enforced with some difficulty. While the New York colony refused to quarter troops, Boston and other colonies unhappily obeyed. Throughout the 1765–1775 period, the Quartering Act was a constant aggravation.

Points of View

Patriots/Radicals: They were angered by the increased presence of troops in the colonies, especially when they were so obviously stationed in places like Boston and New York. In both of these places, opposition was loud. Even the government officials in these colonies opposed the quartering of British troops.

Loyalists: By the year 1770, many Loyalists, or conservatives, were less afraid of the British troops in their midst than they were of the mobs and the Radicals who now appeared to be the greater threat to peace and stability. The "partnership of the Conservatives and Radicals," when they stood shoulder-to-shoulder against the authority of the Crown, was now beginning to fall apart.

Moderates: The farming groups from rural communities were not directly involved or affected by the quartering of troops. They continued to watch and wait, but they were easily swayed by Radicals, who portrayed the Redcoats or members of the British army as the hired bullies of a tyrannical King George III.

The Quartering Act
What Really Happened?

Prime Minister Grenville and Parliament determined that 10,000 British troops would be needed to protect England's American territories. The Proclamation of 1763 was designed to keep settlers out of the West and minimize the numbers of troops that would be needed along the frontier and in outposts. Regardless, soldiers would still be needed. To keep Britain's expenses down, the colonists would quarter the troops when barracks were not available. Public buildings, inns, or similar places, where lodging was available, would also be used. If that did not meet the needs of the local commanders, then vacant houses, barns, or other buildings would be rented. The colonists also had to furnish the troops with supplies. The colonial government would provide reimbursement to the colonists who provided quarters.

From the beginning, the colonists resented the Quartering Act, as it imposed an unwanted military presence. It was the anger and agitation over other Parliamentary acts, however, that brought larger groups of soldiers to America. The ministry ordered a military force to be stationed in Boston. It did not help matters that the Boston officials refused to furnish food and shelter for the arriving troops within the town limits. Radicals like Sam Adams did their best to stir up trouble between the people of Boston and the soldiers. Daily, the British officers and privates were insulted. They were called "Redcoats," "Lobsters," "Bloody Backs," and on many occasions were hit with stones, oyster shells, and snowballs.

There were many Boston businessmen, and other men of wealth and property, who feared and hated the rebel mobs more than they did the soldiers. Unfortunately, these conservative groups lacked the power to prevent the trouble that was brewing. On March 5, 1770, an on-duty British guard near the customhouse was repeatedly bullied by a crowd and pelted with snowballs. The guard called for assistance, and when a sergeant and six men responded, they, too, were abused and attacked. Captain Preston, the commander of the guard, tried to keep control of the situation. The soldiers stood their ground under a heavy shower of snowballs, sticks, and stones, but when a soldier was struck by a club and fell, the British troops opened fire. Three of the mob men were killed outright, and several others were wounded. This incident became known as the Boston Massacre. It was effectively portrayed in an engraving by Paul Revere and used by Sam Adams and his Radical friends to arouse anger throughout the colonies.

The Stamp Act
Just the Facts

Date: 1765

Provisions of the Law

- All commercial and legal documents, liquor licenses, pamphlets, newspapers, almanacs, advertisements, playing cards, and dice required papers with stamped engravings valued from a halfpenny to 10 pounds.

- Violators of the act faced heavy fines, and forgery and counterfeiting were punishable by death.

Reasons for the British Action

- Prime Minister George Grenville wanted the colonies to be responsible for half of the estimated 300,000 pounds needed to protect Britain's American territories. A third of that cost would be covered by the direct tax called for in the Act.

- Grenville welcomed alternative proposals a year before the Act was put into place, but none were forthcoming.

How the Stamp Act Was Enforced

The Act was enforced with great difficulty. It was the Radical group—that is, the poor and those who did not have the right to vote—who protested the most. Royal tax collectors were bullied. Many of the tax collectors were forced to resign. Houses were destroyed by mobs and then burned to the ground. The stamped paper was burned and destroyed. The mobs went wild with anger, and because of this, very little effort was made to collect the tax.

Points of View

Patriots/Radicals: The Radical group (the poorer groups and those who did not have the right to vote) organized themselves into societies that called themselves Sons of Liberty and Daughters of Liberty. Patriots held the Stamp Act Congress in 1765. This Congress, with delegates, or representatives, from nine of the colonies, declared that the colonists could not be denied the basic rights of Englishmen, namely trial by jury, the right of petition, and self-taxation. It requested, through petition, that Parliament and the king repeal the Stamp Act and other obnoxious laws. One of the resolutions of the Stamp Act Congress was that colonists would boycott British goods. As a way of taking a firm stance against the British taxation, merchants agreed not to purchase goods from England.

Loyalists: They trembled with fear and anxiety and resented the violence of the radical mobs.

Moderates: They adopted a wait-and-see attitude.

The Stamp Act
What Really Happened?

A storm broke when news of the Stamp Act reached America's shores. Those upon whom the tax fell most heavily—the merchants, bankers, lawyers, newspaper publishers, and pamphleteers—were the most outspoken in opposing this law. A Stamp Act Congress was called in 1765. Nine of the colonies sent delegates. A great deal of speeches took place. Several representatives listed the basic rights of Englishmen and asked that the Stamp Act end. They stated that only colonial legislatures could tax the colonists. Other colonial leaders also disapproved of the Stamp Act and felt that the actions of Parliament were tyrannical.

Had the colonists only made speeches, held meetings, or written articles, very little would have been accomplished and the Stamp Act would have remained. However, the colonial merchants agreed that as long as such a horrible law was in existence, they would stop buying and importing British goods. The idea of a boycott spread rapidly throughout the colonies. Businessmen in England felt the impact, profits plunged, and the sale of British goods dropped dramatically. Soon, British merchants and businessmen were screaming at members of Parliament to repeal the Stamp Act.

The poorer, lower classes in the colonies gave the king and Parliament the biggest reason to halt their actions. They organized into groups called the *Sons of Liberty* and *Daughters of Liberty* and took to the streets to express their anger. When the call came for action, these unruly mobs were made up of people of all ages who poured out of the shops and the workplaces of the towns. At times, their own members led them, and at other times, they had leaders from the upper classes. They held parades, protesting loudly against the unfair taxation and attacked tax collectors, beating them mercilessly. Some were even "tarred and feathered. Hot tar was poured over their bodies (sometimes killing them), and then they were covered with feathers. After being abused, they were then forced out of town. The mobs burned the stamps whenever they could get their hands on them. They also burned down the homes and destroyed the property of those who were appointed to sell the stamped paper. The violence touched all the colonies and spread rapidly, bordering on outright rebellion.

The boycotts hurt the British merchants in their pocketbooks. As a result of the financial impact combined with the spreading violence throughout colonial society, the king and Parliament repealed the Stamp Act.

The Declaratory Act
Just the Facts

Date: 1766

Provisions of the Law

- It openly declared that Parliament had authority over the colonies.
- This declaration included Parliament's right to tax the colonies.
- The declaration also gave Parliament the right to make laws "to bind the colonies in all cases whatsoever."

Reasons for the British Action

- Parliament insisted it had the right to administer the colonies in whatever fashion it chose.
- Parliament declared the colonies could be taxed to pay their fair share of the expense of Britain's defense of the colonies.

How the Declaratory Act Was Enforced

The colonists did not even notice when the Declaratory Act was passed. They were too busy honoring the king and enjoying the fact that the Stamp Act had been repealed. This Act was just Great Britain's way of saying that they had the right to tax the colonists.

Points of View

Patriots/Radicals: The Radicals, who were too preoccupied with celebrating the end of other British imposed laws, largely ignored this Act of Parliament. The Declaratory Act managed to slip by without the colonists knowing what was happening; they simply weren't paying attention.

Loyalists: They, too, were largely unaware of the measure that was passed by Parliament.

Moderates: They were as unaware as the Patriots and the Loyalists.

The Declaratory Act
What Really Happened?

England miscalculated the rebellious strength of the colonists when it sought to impose the Stamp Act on the American colonies in 1765. The colonists' anger and the demonstrations rapidly grew into open violence. The boycott of British goods, in combination with the post-war (French and Indian War) depression, greatly reduced trade between England and its American colonies to a trickle. It was the merchant class and the businessmen in Britain who screamed the loudest for repealing the Stamp Act. The king and his ministers were unhappy about the course of events, regarding the American colonists as ungrateful. The repeal of the Stamp Act was made bearable because Parliament was able to sneak in the Declaratory Act.

While the colonists were celebrating the end of the Stamp Act, Parliament passed a law that openly repeated England's right to rule and tax the colonies as it pleased. The boycott and the Sons of Liberty forced the repeal of the Stamp Act, but Parliament was determined to have the last word on ruling and taxing the American colonies when it passed the Declaratory Act. The end of the Stamp Tax generated among the American colonists a feeling of good will toward King George III, who was highly praised for his kindness and generosity. Good cheer was felt throughout the colonies—so much so that no one noticed what Parliament had done when it passed the Declaratory Act.

The Townshend Acts
Just the Facts

Date: 1767

Provisions of the Law

- It placed duties on glass, lead, paint, tea, and paper.
- Money was used for paying justices and supporting the civil governments.
- It authorized *Writs of Assistance*, that allowed general search warrants for any reason.
- Smugglers were tried in courts without juries.
- The New York Assembly was suspended for opposing the Quartering Act.

Reasons for the British Action

- Townshend, the British chancellor of the exchequer (the government department in charge of finances), was determined to raise money to ease the burden of war debts.
- Townshend wanted the old Navigation Acts strictly enforced.
- The king, Parliament, and England wanted America to pay a share since Britain had expelled France from the colonies.

★ ★ ★

How the Townshend Acts Were Enforced

England increased the military establishment in America. England was collecting 1,700 pounds in cash from the colonists. However, it cost 7,600 pounds to support the soldiers and royal officials who collected it from the colonists.

Points of View

Patriots/Radicals: They immediately took action. "No taxation without representation" became a slogan that echoed throughout the colonies. Boycotts of British goods were demanded. Colonists refused to pay their taxes. The Sons of Liberty actively opposed royal authorities.

Loyalists: The conservative groups were still in agreement with the Radicals, especially when they opposed British taxes, but caution and anxiety among Loyalists was beginning to set in as they saw mobs in the streets growing in strength and the lower classes gaining greater influence in the communities.

Moderates: They continued their wait-and-see attitude. They accepted the Radical point of view but viewed the mobs with distrust.

The Townshend Acts
What Really Happened?

Events unfolded rapidly in the colonies with the passage of the Townshend Acts. If Prime Minister Grenville's Stamp Act angered the colonists, the Townshend Acts filled them with rage. The cry of "No taxation without representation" echoed throughout colonial assemblies and legislatures, debating halls, and town streets. To the American colonists, the Townshend Acts were the actions of a tyrant. The *Writs of Assistance* (general search warrants) gave the king's men authority to search houses and seize goods for any reason. The Acts allowed smugglers to be tried in courts without juries. Money from the taxes would pay for the administration of colonial governments, taking the "power from the colonists and from their legislatures." The Acts also shut down the New York Assembly, so that it couldn't make laws. This was New York's punishment for disobeying the Quartering Act. Bankruptcies became a common occurrence in the colonies, and the scarcity (lack) of money reached alarming levels. The restrictions that were being placed on the colonies by the king and Parliament only resulted in disobedience and weakened trade. The colonists were not concerned with England's financial problems. The majority of Americans saw England's Acts as sneaky attempts to not only destroy their economy but also to put an end to all of their freedoms and rights.

The most effective weapon the colonists possessed was the boycott of England's merchandise. Colonists agreed not to purchase certain British goods, and many turned eagerly to home manufacturing to provide for their needs. Harvard's students wore homespun material and wrote on paper manufactured in a nearby Massachusetts town. Boston took the lead, and by 1769, Philadelphia, New York, and other smaller commercial centers were doing the same. Some of the Virginia planters, with George Washington at their head, also figured out manufacturing alternatives so colonists would not have to go without supplies.

England's response was to send more troops to America. This single action would further aggravate the colonists. The constant presence of troops only increased the hostility between the colonists and the authorities. It was, finally, the combination of the boycott and the agreements to manufacture their own goods for themselves that brought some action. The growing violence, plus the cost of maintaining a military establishment in America, resulted in the repeal of the Townshend Acts.

The Tea Act
Just the Facts

Date: 1773

Provisions of the Law

- It allowed the British East India Company (BEIC) to become the number-one tea merchant and seller in America.
- The British and colonial importers—the middlemen—were eliminated.
- The BEIC was required to pay a small customs tax.
- The BEIC had no competition and were able to undersell colonial dealers and smugglers by 25 percent.

Reasons for the British Action

- The tea tax would bring in money for the king.
- It would also help the British East India Company get rid of 17 million pounds of excess tea in their warehouses and thereby avoid bankruptcy.

How the Tea Act Was Enforced

The Tea Act was not enforced! In Boston, the Sons of Liberty dumped more than 300 chests of the king's tea into the Boston Harbor. Colonists in Philadelphia refused to allow the ships to unload. In New York, the tea ended up in the East River. In Charleston, South Carolina, the tea was stored in warehouses, and when the conflict between England and its colonies resulted in open fighting, the stored tea was sold at auctions and the profits were used to finance regiments in Washington's army.

Points of View

Patriots/Radicals: Of course, the same cry of "No taxation without representation" was heard. The merchants were not prepared to allow the BEIC to have a monopoly, or exclusive rights, for selling anything: "A tea monopoly today, what tomorrow?" For Sam Adams, it was simply another huge mistake on the part of the British and another reason for the Radicals to resist British rule. As a way of boycotting the Tea Act and the heavy restrictions and taxes that came along with it, the radical group called Sons of Liberty dumped more than 90,000 pounds of tea into the Boston Harbor. This event came to be known as the Boston Tea Party.

Loyalists: They were shocked that the Radicals would dare to destroy the king's tea. Property was sacred!

Moderates: They weren't too happy with the dumping of the tea into the harbor. That smelled of trouble, and many were frightened by the mobs. They were sure it would lead to conflict.

The Tea Act
What Really Happened?

The town of Boston was humming with activity. What was unusual about the Boston Tea Party, however, was that it took place late at night when most townspeople should have been at home behind locked doors and safely in bed. That night, it seemed as if everyone was rushing down to the waterfront. There was a current of excitement in the air! It was a feeling of anticipation that lured people out into the streets. There was talk that tonight, decisive action would take place.

Ever since the Tea Act was passed in 1773, hostilities had been nearing the boiling point. The colonists did not appreciate the British East India Company being given a monopoly, or an exclusive right, to sell their tea in America. Furthermore, the tax on the tea was as disagreeable as any that England had imposed over the past decade.

Sam Adams organized his Sons of Liberty as soon as the ships bringing the tea from England anchored in Boston Harbor. The patriots did not want the tea to be unloaded. The Sons of Liberty could not have asked for a better night. December 16, 1773 turned out to be mild in temperature for that time of year that allowed even more people to join the massive boycott in the Boston Harbor. The moon added brilliance to the scene whenever it peeked out from behind the clouds. Meeting at local taverns, 150 of the Sons of Liberty, mostly Boston's laborers and tradesmen, dressed in costumes thinly disguised as Indians. They boldly marched down the winding streets of Boston, cheered on by the general population.

Rowing out to the three ships anchored in the harbor, they boarded quickly and broke into the compartments where the tea was stored. Hundreds lined the docks and wharves (areas of the harbor where boats go to unload goods). As the sounds of the splintering wood chests echoed across the waters of the harbor, cheers rose to a deafening roar. The Sons of Liberty were breaking the chests and dumping the tea into the dark waters of Boston Harbor. Even the crews of the ships happily joined in the activity, helping to bring the chests on deck and dumping them overboard. Broken chests of tea were flying through the air, and the people of Boston were overjoyed with the excitement of striking a blow for all freemen. Within the hour, there were 342 chests of tea swirling in the currents of Boston Harbor. As quickly as they came, the Sons of Liberty hurried away to their meeting halls, cheered by Bostonians who felt an effective boycott had been enacted against the tyranny of King George III.

The Quebec Act
Just the Facts

Date: 1774

Provisions of the Law

- It established English royal authority in Canada and western territories.
- The French Canadians had most of their ancient rights and customs confirmed.
- The Roman Catholic Church received guarantees against any interference.
- The boundaries of Quebec were extended as far south as the Ohio River and beyond the Allegheny frontier.

Effects of the Law

- It provided that royal authorities would govern over all of Quebec.
- There was to be no elected assembly. No privilege of self-taxation was allowed. No trial by jury was allowed.
- All Catholics were to enjoy religious freedom.

How the Quebec Act Was Enforced

The Quebec Act was never enforced. Within a year, the American colonists were at war with England and ignoring all parts of the Quebec Act. The thirteen colonies did not approve of extending Quebec's boundaries down to the Ohio River. The Americans felt that these were their lands, and they ignored the law.

Points of View

Patriots/Radicals: The Patriots were opposed to the extension of Quebec's boundaries all the way south to the Ohio River. They were also opposed to the land being governed by royal authority. The Radical group also found it insulting that they were not allowed to make their own laws and could not have trial by jury. Finally, the colonial fear of a state-supported Roman Catholic Church was evident, as Americans wanted to ensure freedom of religion.

Loyalists: At this point, the Loyalists were firmly lined up behind the king and royal authority.

Moderates: They were leaning toward the Radical side, but more as a reaction to the Intolerable Acts than the Quebec Act.

The Quebec Act
What Really Happened?

By the time Parliament passed the Quebec Act in 1774, in an effort to put their Canadian affairs in order, the American colonists were immersed in their own problems with England. However, the Quebec Act did not pass completely unnoticed. As with everything else that the British did, the colonists were angered by the decision to extend Quebec's boundaries southward all the way to the Ohio River, including all of the lands west of the Allegheny Mountains. This became a point of distress, for many of the original land grants issued by the king were not clear as far as western boundary lines were concerned.

Many colonies had claims to lands extending westward beyond the Allegheny Mountains. Also, many of these lands were to be set aside for the veterans who had fought in past wars. The colonists viewed the British efforts to restore the French to their ancient customs as sneaky.

The Quebec Act provided that the area would be ruled through British royal authority. True to French traditions, there was no elected assembly, no privilege of self-taxation, and no trial by jury. Within one year, Americans and Englishmen were at war with each other. The Quebec Act was never enforced.

The Intolerable Acts
Just the Facts

Date: 1774

Provisions of the Law

- Martial law (military-run government control of an area after an emergency situation) was imposed in Boston, and the port was closed.
- The Massachusetts Assembly was not allowed to make laws.
- Royal officials who broke the law were to be sent to England for trial.
- The colonists would have to pay for the dumped tea—including the taxes.
- These laws affected none of the other 12 colonies.

Reason for the British Action

- They were meant to punish the people of Boston for destroying the king's tea during the Boston Tea Party.

How the Intolerable Acts Were Enforced

The king appointed General Thomas Gage as Vice Admiral, Captain General, and Governor in Chief of Massachusetts. Boston and all lands stretching inland from it passed from civil rule to military occupation. The king sent more men to the 14th and 29th military regiments. No shipping moved either into or out of Boston. Nearly all government officials were now appointed directly by the king instead of elected by the people. Town meetings could be held only with royal approval, and the discussion planned for each meeting had to be approved beforehand. The capitol (main government building) was moved. All taxes and money collected for duties were now collected by the military. The atmosphere was tense, and people were continually agitated.

Points of View

Patriots/Radicals: They were outraged! Many colonists began to voice the idea of declaring independence. Patriots called for a meeting. At the First Continental Congress, they decided that Massachusetts would form its own government and collect taxes, withholding them from England until the Intolerable Acts were cancelled.

Loyalists: They maintained loyalty to England and opposed the "mobs" of Boston. They supported the payment for the tea.

Moderates: There was a marked shift to the patriot side. If the king and Parliament could take these measures against the citizens of Boston and take away their basic rights, what would be next?

The Intolerable Acts
What Really Happened?

One result of the Intolerable Acts that England never bargained for was the unified opposition of the thirteen colonies. Never before had the colonies taken such a united stand together. The second unexpected result was the open defiance. The other colonies came to the aid of Boston, some with money and others with food and supplies that were smuggled in overland. The harsh law enforced by Parliament to humble Boston never achieved its goal; it only stiffened the determination of the Patriots and Radicals, who were soon preparing to defend themselves against the tyranny of the king. Powder and shot (gunpowder and lead muskets) were stored in villages, far from the reach of the soldiers stationed in Boston. On the village greens, Minutemen practiced their drills, and throughout the countryside, farmers formed militias and armed themselves for the eventuality of defending their homes.

The Radical group controlled the gathering of the First Continental Congress. At the meeting in September 1774, the conservatives were badly outnumbered and badly outsmarted. A statement was issued that set forth a Declaration of American Rights. The Congress also created the Association (First Continental Congress) to stop colonists from buying goods, selling goods, and using goods made in England.

In all of the colonies, the Radicals gained the upper hand. From New Hampshire to the Carolinas, the Association was unanimously approved. Committees were established across the colonies to enforce the Association's rules. Some of the loyalists complained that these committees were made up of people who had nothing to lose, dominated by blacksmiths, carpenters, and shoemakers—the lowest of people. Despite the backlash by loyalists, the committees functioned efficiently, and they enforced the Association's rules. By 1775, within a brief period of time, the import trade between the colonies and England was down by 97 percent as compared to the previous year.

In England, voices were raised asking the king and Parliament to consider repeal of the Intolerable Acts and come to an agreement with the American colonies. Unfortunately, the Crown and Lord North's Ministry were determined to crush the American rebellion.

While Parliament listened to and largely ignored the pleas of its own Edmund Burke to find a path of agreement and resolution, the Radicals in the colonies were busy organizing. Extremists were in control on both sides of the Atlantic, but the Americans were determined to stand firm. The spirit of resistance was sweeping across the land. The Association gained in strength. The Loyalists, however, were not united. The Moderates were carefully watching which way the wind would blow.

Name _____ Date _____

Skit Planning Sheet

Name of the Act
Purpose of the Act
In what ways did it affect the colonists?
In what ways did the colonists react?
Describe in detail the results of the Act.

The Plot: Divide the skit into three parts. Write what happens in each part of the skit.

Part 1	Part 2	Part 3
Show the name and purpose of the Act in this part of the skit.	Show how the Act affected the colonists.	Show how the colonists responded and what happened as a result.

Name _____ **Date** _____

Set the Scene

Group Members: _____

_____

Title of the Act: _____

_____

Directions: Plan your skit by answering the questions below.

Theme (The point of the skit is to show . . .)**:** _____

_____

_____

Setting (Where will the skit take place?)**:** _____

_____

_____

List of Actors/Characters: _____

_____

_____

_____

Props/Costumes Needed: _____

_____

_____

_____

Name _____ Date _____

Storyboard the Skit

Group Members: _____

_____

Title of the Act: _____

_____

Directions: How will you show what happens in each part of the skit? Use the chart below to storyboard (draw the sequence of events) the different scenes.

Scenes of the Skit	Storyboard Ideas			
Part 1 Show the name and purpose of the Act in this part of the skit.				
Part 2 Show how the Act affected the colonists.				
Part 3 Show how the colonists responded and what happened as a result of the Act.				

Name _____ Date _____

Keeping Track of the Acts

Directions: Use this graphic organizer to keep track of the Acts presented in each skit. Take notes in the boxes while each group performs.

Name and Purpose of the Act	How did the Act affect the colonists?	How did the colonists react to the Act?
The Proclamation of 1763		
The Sugar Act		
The Colonial Currency Act		

Name _____ Date _____

Keeping Track of the Acts *(cont.)*

Name and Purpose of the Act	How did the Act affect the colonists?	How did the colonists react to the Act?
The Quartering Act		
The Stamp Act		
The Declaratory Act		

Name _____ Date _____

Keeping Track of the Acts (cont.)

Name and Purpose of the Act	How did the Act affect the colonists?	How did the colonists react to the Act?
The Townshend Acts		
The Tea Act		
The Quebec Act		
The Intolerable Acts		

Name _____ Date _____

Skit Assessment

Group Members: _____

_____

Name of the Act: _____

Brief Summary of the Skit: _____

_____

_____

Directions: Circle the number that best describes each criterion for the play.

Criteria	1–2	3–4	5–6	7–8	Comments
Showed the purpose of the Act	Not clear	Somewhat clear	Clear	Very clear	
Showed how the Act affected the colonists	Not clear	Somewhat clear	Clear	Very clear	
Showed how the colonists reacted to the Act	Not clear	Somewhat clear	Clear	Very clear	
All elements were included in the skit (props, setting, actors)	No elements were included	Some elements were included	Most elements were included	Each element was included	
All group members participated in the skit	No members participated in skit	Some members participated in skit	Most members participated in skit	Each member participated in skit	
Total Points:				_____ /40	

Student Glossary Answer Key

1. abstain (v)

To refrain from something by one's own choice.

2. boycott (v)

To act together in abstaining from using, buying, or dealing with as an expression of protest or disfavor or as a means of threat or intimidation; to abstain from or unite with others in abstaining from using, buying, or dealing with.

3. Conservative (n)

Favoring traditional views and values; tending to oppose change; moderate; cautious.

4. defy (v)

To oppose or resist with boldness and assurance; to refuse to submit to or cooperate with.

defiance (n)

Bold resistance to an opposing force or authority.

5. delegate (n)

A person authorized to act as representative for another; a deputy or an agent.

delegation (n)

A group of persons officially elected or appointed to represent another or others.

6. distiller (n)

One that makes alcoholic liquors by the process of distillation.

7. duty (n)

A tax charged by a government, especially on imported goods.

8. grievance (n)

A complaint or protestation based on an unfavorable circumstance.

9. Loyalist (n)

One who maintains loyalty to an established government, political party, or sovereign, especially during war or revolutionary change.

10. mercantilism (n)

The theory and system of political economy prevailing in Europe after the decline of feudalism, based on national policies of accumulating bullion, establishing colonies and a merchant marine, and developing industry and mining to attain a favorable balance of trade.

11. mercenary (n)

Person hired for service in a foreign army.

12. militia (n)

An army composed of ordinary citizen-soldiers rather than professional soldiers or "regulars"; a military force that is not part of a regular army and is subject to report for service in an emergency.

13. Minutemen (n)

Civilians who volunteered to fight the British at a minute's notice. In 1774, the Minutemen became an organized militia.

Student Glossary Answer Key (cont.)

14. Moderate (n)

One who holds or supports moderate views or opinions, especially in politics or religion.

15. Patriot (n)

One who loves, supports, and defends his or her country.

16. petition (n)

A formal written document requesting a right or benefit from a person or group in authority; a formal written application requesting a court hearing for a specific judicial action.

17. quartering (v)

To take up or be assigned lodgings.

18. Radical (n)

One who advocates fundamental or revolutionary changes in current practices, conditions, or institutions; radicals seeking to overthrow the social order.

19. resolution (n)

A course of action determined or decided on; a formal statement of a decision or expression of opinion put before or adopted by an assembly such as the U.S. Congress.

20. servitude (n)

A state of subjection to an owner or a master; the performance of involuntary labor or service for a master.

21. treason (n)

Violation of allegiance toward one's country or sovereign, especially the betrayal of one's country by waging war against it or by consciously and purposely acting to aid its enemies.

22. unanimous (adj)

Having the agreement and consent of all.

Keeping Track of the Acts Answer Key

Name and Purpose of the Act	Name and Purpose of the Act
The Proclamation of 1763 England did not want to spend money defending frontier areas.	**The Sugar Act** England needed to raise money for the treasury. Sugar was taxed; duty on molasses was lowered; the Act outlawed foreign sugar/molasses; a heavy tax on imports was enforced.
How did the Act affect the colonists?	**How did the Act affect the colonists?**
The colonists were not allowed to settle west of the Allegheny Mountains, which was set aside as Indian lands. Settlers already there were told to move and go back to the East.	Restrictions were placed on colonial trade with French and Spanish West Indies. Colonists had to import molasses from the British West Indies, but there wasn't enough to meet the colonists' needs.
How did the colonists react to the Act?	**How did the colonists react to the Act?**
Colonists were angry. Many felt the French and Indian War was fought to eliminate the French from these territories and open them to American settlement. Colonists continued to move West and settle there.	Colonists grumbled, but most obeyed the law while the others continued to smuggle. Sugar and molasses continued to make its way into the colonies through smuggling.

Keeping Track of the Acts Answer Key *(cont.)*

Name and Purpose of the Act	Name and Purpose of the Act
The Colonial Currency Act	**The Quartering Act**
Colonial government was forbidden to print currency; only gold and silver could be used to repay debts.	Colonists were to provide housing, food, and supplies for British troops. The colonists were to be paid by the colonial legislatures.
How did the Act affect the colonists?	**How did the Act affect the colonists?**
Many businesses went into bankruptcy. No French or Spanish gold was coming into the colonies because of the Sugar Act. Cheap money was outlawed.	The presence of British soldiers angered the colonists because they knew the troops were there to enforce the king's laws. Some colonies refused to quarter the troops.
How did the colonists react to the Act?	**How did the colonists react to the Act?**
The colonists continued to trade with the French and Spanish. Smuggling provided the colonies with the silver and gold they needed.	Many of the colonial governments refused to quarter troops. Anger and resentment began to build up among colonists in Boston resulting in the infamous Boston Massacre.

Keeping Track of the Acts Answer Key *(cont.)*

Name and Purpose of the Act	Name and Purpose of the Act
The Stamp Act	**The Declaratory Act**
England wanted to raise money by taxing legal papers, pamphlets, newspapers, etc. with special tax stamps (valued from a halfpenny to 10 pounds).	Parliament canceled the Stamp Act but said it had the right to govern and tax the colonies.
How did the Act affect the colonists?	**How did the Act affect the colonists?**
All legal papers, books, pamphlets, newspapers, and decks of cards were taxed.	This law restated and reinforced Parliament's right and decision to tax and govern the colonies.
How did the colonists react to the Act?	**How did the colonists react to the Act?**
Colonists were angry and hostile. The Sons of Liberty and Daughters of Liberty were organized. The king's tax collectors were beaten and terrorized. Colonists boycotted British goods.	Colonists were too busy celebrating the repeal of the Stamp Act, and the Declaratory Act slipped by unnoticed.

Keeping Track of the Acts Answer Key *(cont.)*

Name and Purpose of the Act	Name and Purpose of the Act
The Townshend Acts To raise money, taxes were placed on items like paint, glass, lead, paper, and tea.	**The Tea Act** It gave the British East India Company (BEIC) a monopoly to sell excess tea in the colonies. The BEIC had a surplus of tea in London warehouses.
How did the Act affect the colonists?	**How did the Act affect the colonists?**
The Townshend Acts provided *Writs of Assistance,* which were search warrants allowing the king's men to search and seize at will.	The colonists resented the BEIC being given an absolute monopoly to sell tea even though it was cheap to buy. Many merchants were also resentful since BEIC tea was even cheaper than smuggled tea.
How did the colonists react to the Act?	**How did the colonists react to the Act?**
Sons of Liberty used violence and demonstrations. British goods were boycotted. The outcry cut across all levels of colonial society, with conservatives and radicals acting together. The Townshend Acts were repealed.	In Boston, they dumped the tea into the harbor, and in New York, it went into the East River. It wasn't even unloaded in Philadelphia, and it was warehoused in Charleston.

Keeping Track of the Acts Answer Key (cont.)

Name and Purpose of the Act	Name and Purpose of the Act
The Quebec Act	**The Intolerable Acts**
This Act was put in place to settle problems in Canada. It allowed the French their customs and traditional ways of life.	King George III and Parliament wanted to punish Boston for the Boston Tea Party.
How did the Act affect the colonists?	**How did the Act affect the colonists?**
The Quebec Act extended the provincial boundaries to north of the Ohio River and west of the Allegheny Mountains. This angered colonists.	Boston came under martial law. The British closed the port of Boston. General Gage became the governor, and England now appointed all government officials.
How did the colonists react to the Act?	**How did the colonists react to the Act?**
French practices and customs did not provide for self-governing legislatures or trial by jury. Recognizing Catholicism raised the unlikable idea of a state religion.	The colonies joined together in opposition to the British. Colonists supplied Boston with food and provisions. The colonies called the First Continental Congress.

Making Mystery Boxes

Objectives

- Students will use a variety of sources to create an accurate and balanced picture of an individual whose actions impacted the American Revolution. Using the inquiry approach to research, students will examine the life of one key figure.
- Students will create Mystery Boxes and write short essays about their figures to share their learning.
- Students will examine, interpret, and interact with one another's projects.

Standards

- McREL United States History Level II, 6.5
- CCSS.ELA-Literacy.CCRA.R.3
- CCSS.ELA-Literacy.CCRA.W.9

Materials List

- Reproducibles (pages 66–76)
- Primary and secondary source materials about the American Revolution
- Sample Mystery Box
- Internet access
- Shoeboxes with lids
- Markers/colored pencils
- Index cards

Overarching Essential Question

What is independence?

Guiding Questions

- In what ways did revolutionary leaders have an effect on the events leading to the revolution?
- Describe in detail the influence that ordinary colonists had on the impending conflict.
- The American Colonies were established with the intent of having a democratic government. For what reasons were ordinary people's voices so critical in making a revolution?
- Explain specifically the key players and their contributions to the American Revolution. In what ways did they or did they not achieve success?

Suggested Schedule

The schedule below is based on a 45-minute period. If your school has block scheduling, please modify the schedule to meet your own needs.

Day 1	Day 2	Day 3	Day 4	Day 5	Day 6
Introductory Writing Activity Students will **learn how to write creative introductions.**	Each student **selects an individual** and **prepares questions** for the research process.	Students continue to **research** and **write introductions.**	Students **create mystery boxes** for their selected individuals.	Students **play** the Mystery Box Game.	Students **sort** the famous individuals into categories and **write reflections** on the essential question.

Making Mystery Boxes *(cont.)*

Day 1
Introductory Activity

1. Begin by explaining that introductions are really short biographies about a person. Have the class brainstorm ways of creatively introducing themselves. Write down ideas on the board. Offer a few ideas to get students started, such as:

   • Use an acrostic poem with adjectives that describe you based on your name.

   • List the five Ws about you in a very brief way (*who, what, when, where, why*).

   • Begin with a strange question like "Do people find your name weird?"

2. Have students search online for creative examples to add to the list. For example, students can search using the terms *creative blogger bio pages*. Many people give short biographies about themselves on websites, blogs, and the backs of books.

3. Have students write creative introductions about themselves on index cards using the techniques they saw and the ideas listed during the brainstorming session. They can also use the compiled list on the *Creative Introductions* sheet (page 66).

Day 2

1. Copy the *Calling Cards from the American Revolution* sheet (pages 67–69), cut them apart, and place them in a hat or a bag. Each card gives a brief biography about an important figure from the time period.

2. Explain that long ago, calling cards introduced someone when they arrived as a guest at someone's house. In the same way, they will be introduced to a person from the time of the American Revolution. Have each student draw a card from the hat or bag.

3. Tell students that they will complete an in-depth research project on the person listed on the card they selected. They will write mini biographies, or introductions, create a Mystery Box, and play the Mystery Box Game.

4. Place students in small groups and have them work together to make a list of general questions they would like to answer as they research their subjects. The teacher-coach roams the room offering guidance and assistance. Invite students to share their ideas with the class. Record students' ideas on the board or on chart paper.

Making Mystery Boxes (cont.)

5. Distribute copies of the *Inquiring Minds* sheet (page 70) to students. Ask students to choose the questions from the class list or from their group lists that they want to answer in their research. Have them organize the questions into the two categories on the activity sheet.

Days 2–3

1. Distribute copies of the *Writing Introductions* sheet (page 72) to students. Review the instructions with students. Fill out the Points Possible column of the *Introductions Rubric* sheet (page 73) and review the expectations with students, using negotiable contracting.

2. Discuss primary sources with students. Share and analyze examples of primary sources. Require students to read or view at least one primary source in their research. This could be in the form of a letter, a poster, a speech, or an image. A *Primary Source Analysis* sheet (page 71) can be distributed to help students better understand primary sources.

3. Provide time for students to research their subjects and write their introductions. Students may need to complete their research and introductions outside class. Roam the room offering guidance and assistance.

Day 4

1. Distribute copies of the *How to Make a Mystery Box* sheet (page 74) to students. Review the instructions with students. Fill out the *Points Possible* column of the *Mystery Box Project Rubric* (page 75) and review the expectations with students. Present a sample Mystery Box from years past as an example to help students understand what is needed to design a Mystery Box.

2. Provide time for students to make their Mystery Boxes. Students may need additional time outside the classroom to complete their boxes.

Day 5

1. After students have turned in their completed projects, have them play the Mystery Box Game. Divide the class into groups of four.

2. Have each group set up a station for their Mystery Boxes. Tell each group to mix their introduction index cards together and leave them with the Mystery Boxes.

3. Have the groups rotate to different stations to play the game so that the new station offers boxes that have not been seen before. Distribute a copy of the *Mystery Box Game Chart* sheet (page 76) to each student.

Making Mystery Boxes (cont.)

4. Model the strategy to students before they begin. Group members will work together to match the index cards with the correct Mystery Boxes. Group members should take turns drawing index cards from the pile and reading them aloud. The group will discuss where each card belongs based on the decorative clues on the Mystery Box. They will drop the cards into the slots on top of the correct boxes. Remind students that each box should have only four cards.

5. After each card has been placed in a Mystery Box, each student will open one of the Mystery Boxes. Students will reread the index cards silently and put them in chronological order. Students will then guess the names of each Mystery Box. Encourage group members to work together. Ask students what they will be observing while they play the game, as a form of performance assessment.

6. To check their guesses, students can flip over the index cards and the boxes. The quotations on the cards and the bottoms of the boxes should match. The quotation should help students to verify their guesses. Students can find out the correct subject by lifting the flap on the inside bottom of the box to find the name.

7. Have students complete the *Mystery Box Game Chart* (page 76) to compile the information they learned from all four subjects/people. You may choose to repeat this process for another round or two so students have opportunities to learn about many of the important figures of the American Revolution.

Day 6

1. Divide the class into small groups. Distribute the *Calling Cards from the American Revolution* (pages 67–69) to each group. Make sure the pages are not copied front and back.

2. Instruct students to cut the cards apart.

3. Challenge students to use what they learned from their classmates' Mystery Boxes to sort the people into categories. Groups should invent their own categories and write them as headings. Then they should take the headings and place them in a pile.

4. Rotate all groups and have the new group look at the information and guess the categories by placing the proper heading on the chart.

5. Provide time for groups to share and justify their category choices.

6. Write the guiding questions from the unit on the board or on chart paper. Have students form small groups and discuss the question as a reflection and what it meant to them personally.

7. After a few minutes of discussion, have students write a paragraph ticket-out-the-door that gives their best answer to the guiding question.

Name _____ Date _____

Creative Introductions

Directions: Below are ideas for creative introductions. These can be spoken, written, or shown visually. Use these to help you write your creative introduction.

Discuss with students the notion of clichés and stereotypes of the times and how they feel that they either fit them or don't fit them.

- Answer the question: *Who am I?* in one sentence.

- A little bit about me … (Have a creative picture showing only half your face.)

- Briefly list the 5 Ws about yourself.

- Begin with something mysterious: "Who is this man? Artist, myth, or mega designer?"

- Make a list of things found in your trash and what they can that tell about you.

- Draw a time line and predict things that might happen (This person will probably ___ on ___).

- Begin with a strange question: "Do people find your name weird?"

- Refer to yourself in hero/heroine fashion and tell it like a story: "Fast forward three years, we find our hero . . ."

- Offer a strange picture of yourself in action and give a caption about something you do (For example: *Sometimes sings*).

- Introduce yourself with a nickname that tells something about who you are (For example: *The unstoppable ninja warrior*).

- Draw a cartoon caricature and point to features that tell something about yourself. Add comments.

- Have a picture of your body with a smiley face box on your head to conceal your identity.

Calling Cards from the American Revolution

Directions: Cut apart the cards and have students use them to complete the research project.

Abigail Smith Adams — The American colonist and patriot who was an early advocate for women's rights; she was the wife of President John Adams and the mother of President John Quincy Adams	**John Adams** — The American colonist, patriot, and Founding Father; he was the first U.S. Vice President and the second U.S. President
Samuel Adams — An American colonist, patriot, and Founding Father; Thomas Jefferson said that he was "truly the Man of the Revolution"	**Ethan Allen** — A commander of the Green Mountain Boys militia; he led the capture of Fort Ticonderoga early in the Revolutionary War
Benedict Arnold — A general in the Continental Army who fought bravely at Saratoga; betrayed the colonies and later became a British Army officer	**Crispus Attucks** — An American slave who became the first casualty of the American Revolution when he was killed during the Boston Massacre
Chief Joseph Brant — A Mohawk Indian chief who served as a British officer in the American Revolution	**General John Burgoyne** — A British Army general who surrendered to the Continental Army at the Battle of Saratoga
Aaron Burr — An officer in the Continental Army and U.S. politician; third vice president of the U.S. government; killed Alexander Hamilton in a duel	**George Rogers Clark** — The highest-ranking Continental Army officer on the northwestern frontier in the American Revolution; he was called the *Conqueror of the Old Northwest*
General Charles Cornwallis — A British Army general who surrendered to the Continental Army at the Battle of Yorktown	**Benjamin Franklin** — An American colonist, patriot, and Founding Father; he was also a writer, a publisher, an inventor, and a diplomat

Calling Cards from the American Revolution (cont.)

General Thomas Gage — A British Army general in the American Revolution; earned a bloody and hollow victory at Bunker Hill	**Horatio Gates** — A Continental Army General in the American Revolution; he played a role in the controversial Conway Cabal
George Grenville — The British Prime Minister and author of the Stamp Act	**Nathan Hale** — A school teacher; Continental Army soldier who was hanged as a spy by the British
Alexander Hamilton — A Continental Army officer, George Washington's aide, and the creator of the new nation's economic policies	**John Hancock** — A wealthy American merchant, patriot, and Founding Father; he was famous for his large signature on the Declaration of Independence; he went on to become the governor of Massachusetts
Mary Ludwig Hays — An American patriot nicknamed Molly Pitcher; she fought in the Battle of Monmouth after her husband was wounded	**Patrick Henry** — An American colonist, patriot, and Founding Father; a gifted speaker who is famous for his "Give me liberty or give me death!" speech
General William Howe — A British Army general during the American Revolution who, when he had the opportunity, inexplicably failed to destroy Washington's army	**Thomas Jefferson** — An American colonist, patriot, and Founding Father; the author of the Declaration of Independence
John Paul Jones — An officer in the Continental Navy during the American Revolution; he was famous for his tenacity and bravery in battle; "I have not yet begun to fight"	**James Madison** — An American colonist, patriot, and Founding Father; wrote the Bill of Rights to the Constitution of 1787; he was the fourth U.S. President
Francis Marion — An officer in the Continental Army during the American Revolution; he was called Swamp Fox for his guerilla warfare tactics in the southern campaigns	**Thomas Paine** — An American patriot and author of the influential pamphlet *Common Sense*, also *The Crisis*; his writing convinced many to support independence

Calling Cards from the American Revolution (cont.)

Major John Pitcairn	A British Marine officer who died in the Battle of Bunker Hill	**Charles Wilson Peale**	A Continental Army soldier and painter; he was famous for his portraits of leaders of the American Revolution
Edmund Randolph	An American patriot and politician from Virginia; he introduced the Virginia Plan; he was the first U.S. Attorney General	**Paul Revere**	An American patriot famous for his midnight ride to warn the militia at Lexington and Concord of the British Army's approach
Betsy Ross	An American patriot who sewed the first American flag	**Deborah Sampson**	A soldier in the Continental Army who disguised herself as a man in order to fight
Daniel Shays	An American patriot and leader of Shays' Rebellion against taxes in Massachusetts	**John Stark**	An officer in the Continental Army; led the Green Mountain Boys at the Battle of Bennington
Baron von Steuben	A Prussian-born military officer who taught the Continental Army how to fight; he was one of the fathers of the Continental Army	**Mercy Otis Warren**	An American patriot and political writer
George Washington	An American patriot, Commander in Chief and Continental Army general; the first U.S. President	**Phillis Wheatley**	An American patriot and playwright; the first African American poet and first African American woman to publish a book
James Wilkinson	A Continental Army soldier and American politician; a corrupt scoundrel later found to be spying for Spain		

Name _____ Date _____

Inquiring Minds

Directions: Think about the questions that will guide your research. Organize your questions into the two categories below.

Questions I Must Answer	Questions I Would Like to Answer

Name _____ **Date** _____

Primary Source Analysis

Directions: Answer the following questions about the primary sources you find in your research.

1. What type of primary source is this?

   _____

   _____

2. Describe in detail the primary source. Include any interesting or unique characteristics.

   _____

   _____

   _____

3. Explain specifically what the primary source tells you about the American Revolution. (Include explicit and implicit information.)

   _____

   _____

   _____

4. Describe in detail the purpose of this item.

   _____

   _____

5. Who was the intended audience or user of this item?

   _____

6. Describe in detail what the primary source tells you about life in America during this time period. (Include explicit and implicit information.)

   _____

   _____

   _____

Name _____ Date _____

Writing Introductions

1. Let the list of questions you generated on the *Inquiring Minds* sheet (page 70) be your guide. Use books, the Internet, and primary-source documents to find out as much as possible about your subject. Try to keep your subject secret. You must complete your research by _____ .

2. An introduction to a person is similar to writing a mini biography. Compile your research into a four-paragraph introduction of the person Do NOT use the subject's name. Replace the name with pronouns and appositives, such as *he, she, the man, the woman, the patriot, the soldier,* and *the leader*. Use transition words that provide clues as to the order of the paragraphs, such as *to start with, next, secondly, also, in addition,* and *finally*.

3. Work with a partner to peer-edit each other's introductions. Check for clarity, organization, creative use of language, and interesting details.

4. Type the final draft of the introduction. All students need to use one simple, readable font (for example, Black, Times New Roman, 12-point font). Set up the page with two-inch margins. Add an extra space between paragraphs.

5. Cut the final draft apart so that each paragraph is separate. Glue each paragraph onto an index card.

6. Think of a famous quote or clever saying that provides a clue about the identity of your subject. If Paul Revere is your subject, you might choose, *"The British are coming!"*

7. Put the index cards in order from left to right. Turn the index cards face-down. Write the quote so that one or two words are on each card. Players will use this clue during the Mystery Box Game.

Name _____ Date _____

Introductions Rubric

Criteria	1–2	3–4	5–6	7–8
Sources	Information is not gathered from a variety of sources	Some information is gathered from a variety of sources	All information is gathered from a variety of sources	Detailed information is gathered from a variety of sources
Information	Introduction does not follow assignment guidelines	Introduction somewhat follows assignment guidelines	Introduction accurately follows assignment guidelines	Introduction accurately follows assignment guidelines and has great detail
Accuracy	Facts and details in introduction are not accurate	Facts and details in the introduction are somewhat accurate	Facts and details in the introduction are accurate	Facts and details in the introduction are accurate and detailed
Introduction	Introduction is not informative and interesting	Introduction is somewhat informative and interesting	Information is informative and interesting	Introduction is informative, interesting, and includes great detail
Peer Editing	Student does not participate in effective peer editing	Student somewhat participates in effective peer editing	Student participates in effective peer editing	Student participates very effectively in peer editing
Final Draft	Final draft is not complete	Final draft is somewhat complete	Final draft is complete	Final draft is completed in great detail
Quote	No quote is included or is not appropriate for the Mystery Box clue	Quote is somewhat appropriate for Mystery Box clue	Quote is appropriate for Mystery Box clue	Quote is very appropriate for Mystery Box clue

Comments and Total Points: /56 pts.

Name _____ Date _____

How to Make a Mystery Box

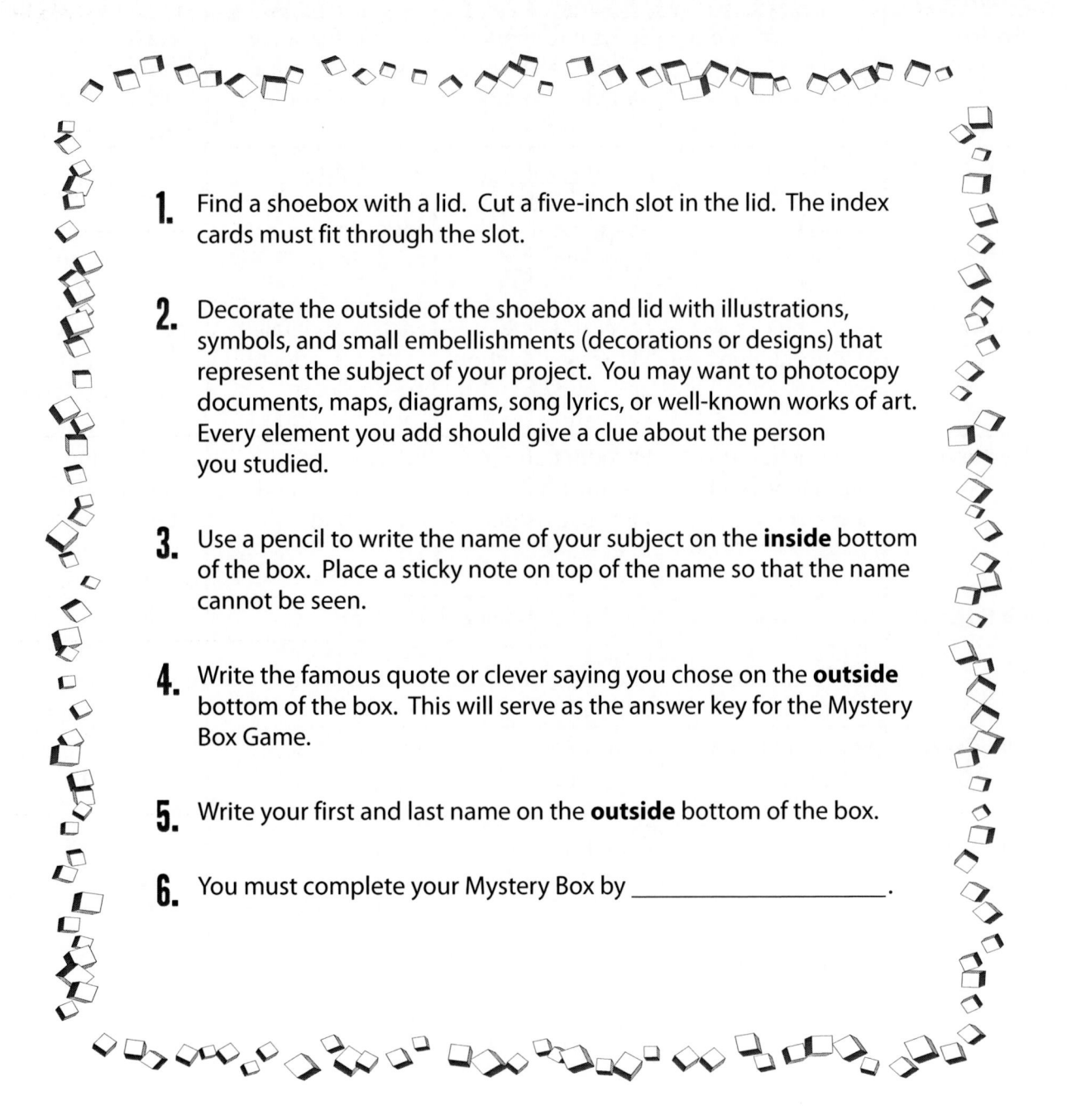

1. Find a shoebox with a lid. Cut a five-inch slot in the lid. The index cards must fit through the slot.

2. Decorate the outside of the shoebox and lid with illustrations, symbols, and small embellishments (decorations or designs) that represent the subject of your project. You may want to photocopy documents, maps, diagrams, song lyrics, or well-known works of art. Every element you add should give a clue about the person you studied.

3. Use a pencil to write the name of your subject on the **inside** bottom of the box. Place a sticky note on top of the name so that the name cannot be seen.

4. Write the famous quote or clever saying you chose on the **outside** bottom of the box. This will serve as the answer key for the Mystery Box Game.

5. Write your first and last name on the **outside** bottom of the box.

6. You must complete your Mystery Box by _____.

Name _____ Date _____

Mystery Box Project Rubric

Criteria	Bronze (Level I)	Silver (Level II)	Gold (Level III)	Platinum (Level IV)	
Project Guidelines	Mystery Box did not meet project guidelines (1–2 pts.)	Mystery Box somewhat met project guidelines (3–4 pts.)	Mystery Box met project guidelines (5–6 pts.)	Mystery box met project guidelines in detail (7–8 pts.)	/8
Design	Completed product is not original (1–4 pts.)	Completed product includes some originality (5–8 pts.)	Completed product is original (9–12 pts.)	Completed project original and has great detail (13–16 pts.)	/16
Finished Product	Completed product in not neat and attractive (1–4 pts.)	Completed product is somewhat neat and attractive (5–8 pts.)	Completed product is neat and attractive (9–12 pts.)	Completed product is exceptional in neatness and attractiveness (13–16 pts.)	/16
Time Management	Time was not used efficiently (1–2 pts.)	Time was somewhat used efficiently (3–4 pts.)	Time was adequately used (5–6 pts.)	Time was efficiently used (7–8 pts.)	/8
Comments:					**Total Points:** /48 pts.

Name _____ **Date** _____

Mystery Box Game Chart

Directions: Record the information you learned from the mini biographies and Mystery Boxes.

Person's Name	How was he or she important to the American Revolution?	Other Facts	Remaining Questions

Building Battlefield Tours

Objectives

- Students will work in groups to design audio and pocket travel guides for tourists who visit the different towns where famous revolutionary battles occurred.
- Students will record their tours using audio-recording programs.
- Students will take "tourists" on their audio and pocket guide tours.

Standards

- McREL United States History Level II, 6.4
- CSS.ELA-Literacy.CCRA.R.7
- CSS.ELA-Literacy.CCRA.SL.4

Materials List

- Reproducibles (pages 82, 84–102)
- Teacher Resources (page 83)

Overarching Essential Question

What is independence?

Guiding Questions

- In what ways was the American Revolution a "civil war?"
- Explain specifically how difficult it was to fight your neighbor, when one could be a Loyalist and the other could be a Patriot.
- Describe in detail the influence that revolutionary leaders had on the events leading up to the battles fought in your backyard, so to speak.
- In what ways did the British try to crush the rebellion staged by the colonists?

Suggested Schedule

The schedule below is based on a 45-minute period. If your school has block scheduling, please modify the schedule to meet your own needs.

Day 1	Day 2	Day 3	Day 4	Day 5	Day 6	Day 7
Introductory Activity Students have **American Revolution conversations** to become familiar with the vocabulary.	Students are **introduced to guided tours of historical sites** and **prepare to create** their own pocket guides and audio tours.	Students **begin research** on various battles during the American Revolution.	Students **write their pocket guides**.	Students **write their audio scripts**.	Students **record the audio**.	Students **trade audio tours** and **pocket guides** to learn about the battles during the American Revolution and **complete assessments**.

Building Battlefield Tours *(cont.)*

Introductory Activity

1. Contact the local Chamber of Commerce for areas around the various battle sites and request brochures for walking tours. This type of brochure differs from others, as it asks the reader to look for items (buildings, parks, etc.) as they take a walking tour or a driving tour of the area. Try to obtain some for the class.

2. Obtain guidebooks and pocket guides of famous places. Bookmark famous sites online that advertise how their walking tours work as well as apps for guided tours.

Day 1

1. Distribute copies of the *American Revolution Conversations* sheet (page 82) to students. Give them time to look up how these words were used in context during the time of the American Revolution.

2. Students can check their definitions and understandings of the words with the *American Revolution Conversations Answer Key* sheet (page 83).

3. Have students walk around the room holding conversations, using these words as if they were living during the American Revolution. After each conversation, have the corresponding partner initial next to the words that were used correctly. Encourage students to do this several times, each time creating a different conversation. This way, students will become familiar with all the words and be prepared for the upcoming reading selections. Make a word wall with these words.

Day 2

1. Ask the class if anyone has ever taken a self-guided tour. Let the students describe their experiences.

2. Explain that a tour map typically contains all of the necessary information in order to begin in one area and end in another. It provides pictures, historical information, land formations, and weather conditions that may have affected an event that took place in the past. Share some bookmarked Internet sites with students that explain how their guided tours work. Investigate various apps that assist in tours as well.

Building Battlefield Tours (cont.)

3. Distribute the sample travel guides and ask students to analyze them in their groups by answering the following questions:

    a. Describe in detail the different components of the guide *(e.g., descriptions, directions, pictures, historical information, land formations, seasons).*

    b. Describe specifically the type of language that is used. *(Make sure it's simple and easy to follow, so visiting tourists can understand it. Let them find examples of how important information is explained with precision, using a minimum number of words.)*

    c. In what ways could you improve this guide? *(Encourage students to look at how the maps, pictures, or illustrations complement the text and how they coordinate as a whole.)*

4. Explain to students that they will be creating pocket guides with audio tours about one of five American Revolution battles: Lexington and Concord, New York Campaign, Battle of Trenton, Battle of Saratoga, or Battle of Yorktown.

5. The assignment is twofold: First, students will create pocket guides. Remind students that a pocket guide is a small booklet that can fit in a person's pocket. Then, students will make MP3 recordings that can be played on iPods® or other audio devices that will enhance and elaborate on the information found in the pocket guides.

6. Divide the class into five groups. Assign a different revolutionary battle to each group. Within each group, have students form partners. Each partner group will be creating one pocket guide and one audio recording, resulting in multiple pocket guides for each battle. Students should work together to decide who will focus primarily on the audio recording and who will focus on the pocket guide.

Day 3

1. Distribute copies of the assigned *Battle Descriptions* (pages 84–93), which include text about the battles and the corresponding battle maps.

2. Give students time to read the background and study the map with their partners. Encourage them to make notes and highlight important things on the pages.

3. Students should conduct some research to find out more details about their battle, so they can put it into their pocket guides and audio. Have some available resources, such as encyclopedias, reference books, the Internet, and travel brochures for students to use.

4. For homework, student partner groups should continue to conduct in-depth research on the battle assigned to the group.

Building Battlefield Tours (cont.)

Day 4

1. Have students merge their information with their partners. At this point, embark on the negotiable contracting process, making sure that the students know the criteria that will make their guide outstanding. A rubric can be designed for students using the criteria of assessment.

2. Distribute copies of the *Steps for Making a Pocket Guide* sheet (pages 94–95) and *Organizing the Pocket Guide Information* (page 96) sheets.

3. Students will work together to make a plan for the pocket guide.

4. Students will finish the pocket guides for homework.

★ ★ ★

Day 5

1. Distribute the *Organizing the Audio Recording* (page 97) and *Writing the Audio Script* sheets (pages 98–100) to students.

2. Students will work together to write a script for the audio recording so that it complements the pocket guide. Remind students that they should not record the information written on their pocket guides, but rather, the recorded information should provide more detail. A discussion on how an audio guide is different should be discussed. In what ways does an audio guide make the written text come to life? Sometimes, personal stories or fun factoids can add to the flavor of the recording. For example, the student could pose the question "How much time do you think it took for a militiaman to reload his weapon?"

3. Talk about how students can add sound effects to make their recording come alive as if it were recorded at the actual time of the Revolution. Allow students to experiment with this.

4. Students will finish their scripts for homework.

★ ★ ★

Day 6

1. Allow students time to record their scripts.

2. Encourage them to look back at the checklist to make sure they have met the requirements of the assignment.

3. Those who finish their scripts should upload them to your computer (for example, in your iTunes®). Students will finish their recordings for homework and upload their recordings the next day.

Building Battlefield Tours (cont.)

Day 7

1. Decide how students will listen to their audio recordings. Assign a device to each group with the audio preloaded on it.

2. Have students place their devices with the audio recordings along with their pocket guides around the room.

3. Distribute copies of *The Battles of the American Revolution* sheet (page 101) to students. Students will keep track of what they learn about the battles on this page.

4. Allow students to view pocket guides and listen to the audio about the other battles during the American Revolution. If possible, have students do this in sequential order so that the war makes better sense to them.

5. Based on the negotiable contracting that took place earlier, use the *American Revolution Assessment* (page 102) to assess student pocket guides and audio recordings.

6. Finish your time together by discussing the guiding questions for this lesson and how it applies to what students have learned.

Name _____ Date _____

American Revolution Conversations

Directions: Find out what these words mean and how they were used during the American Revolution. Then, have a conversation with those around you using these words in the context of the American Revolution. An example has been provided for you.

Vocabulary Word	Meaning	Conversation Ideas
Loyalist	One who maintains loyalty to an established government, a political party, or a sovereign, especially during war or revolutionary change.	The loyalists didn't always agree with the radical colonists (e.g., The Quartering Act).
Radicals		
militia		
fortification		
raw militia		
muskets		
alliance		
Tories		

American Revolution Conversations Answer Key

Vocabulary Word	Meaning
Radicals	A term used for colonists—those who advocated extreme measures and actions—who supported the Revolution.
militia	An army made up of self-trained citizen-soldiers, not "regulars," specifically colonists.
fortification	The strengthening of the area around an army by building up fallen trees, dirt, and stones for protection.
raw militia	Those who were recent recruits and especially new compared to the veteran troops of militia who have already been in action.
muskets	Heavy, large infantry weapons; guns used by soldiers before the invention of the lighter rifle and that were not very accurate.
alliance	A formal agreement or pact between two or more countries to reach a certain goal.
Tories	Also called loyalists; an American colonists who supported the British cause in the American Revolution.

Battle Descriptions

Lexington and Concord, 1775

The first blows of the American Revolution were struck on the morning of April 19, 1775. British General Gage, military governor of Massachusetts, sent a flying column (troops on a rapid march) of British soldiers to the small towns of Lexington and Concord. He hoped to arrest two radicals, Samuel Adams and John Hancock, and in the process capture stores of powder and ammunition that were being collected by the local militia.

The midnight ride of Paul Revere and William Dawes wakened the countryside. These two men rode through towns of sleeping colonists yelling, "The British are coming!" When the British soldiers marched into Lexington, small groups of militia, all local farmers, were on the village green. Major John Pitcairn, in command of the British soldiers, rode forward and ordered the Minutemen to break up and disband. In all the confusion, a shot was fired. It has never been determined which side fired first, but when the smoke finally cleared, there were eight villagers lying dead on the ground, many shot in the back as they tried to flee. Some of the wounded farmers were shown no mercy and were killed with bayonets.

The British continued on to Concord. As they marched, the countryside was called to action. What happened at Lexington could be likened to a stone hitting a hornet's nest: angry hornets swarm out in a frenzy to attack an enemy who threatens their dwelling. As the British soldiers approached Concord, the militia was everywhere to the left and to the right but cautiously drew back. The British soldiers searched the houses in Concord and the surrounding farms.

Smoke rose above the trees that shielded Concord from view. It gave the militia the false impression that the British were setting fire to the town. The Minutemen rushed toward the North Bridge, that were fired upon by Redcoats. They returned a volley of fire and saw the British break and run. At that very moment, new soldiers sent by General Gage arrived from Boston to give aid, and the colonists were held back. As the British troop began their retreat, the end of the column of soldiers turned and fired one last volley at the Americans. Apparently fired with venom, this last volley unleashed a fury. It was at this point that the real battle began.

The British soldiers marched in their orderly columns down the same country roads and lanes that had first brought them into the peaceful Massachusetts countryside. The march back to Boston turned into a bloody retreat and a shameful loss. First scores, then hundreds, and finally thousands of angry and defiant Americans were behind every stone wall, barn, shed, woodpile, and tree—all anxious to get a shot at the hated Redcoats as they scurried back to Boston and their barracks.

When the British troops dropped down in exhaustion beneath the sheltering guns of the Royal Navy in Boston Harbor, only then were they safe. General Gage reported 72 killed.

It may seem astonishing that the casualties among the British were so light. Yet it must be remembered that the Americans were farmers, shopkeepers, laborers, and townspeople—not trained soldiers or long-rifle hunters from the frontier. What is important is that they answered the call of duty. Many went home after the day's events, but many remained ready for battle and formed the core of a new army that would experience the rites of passage through Trenton, Ticonderoga, Saratoga, King's Mountain, and Yorktown.

Battle Descriptions *(cont.)*

Lexington and Concord

National Park Service

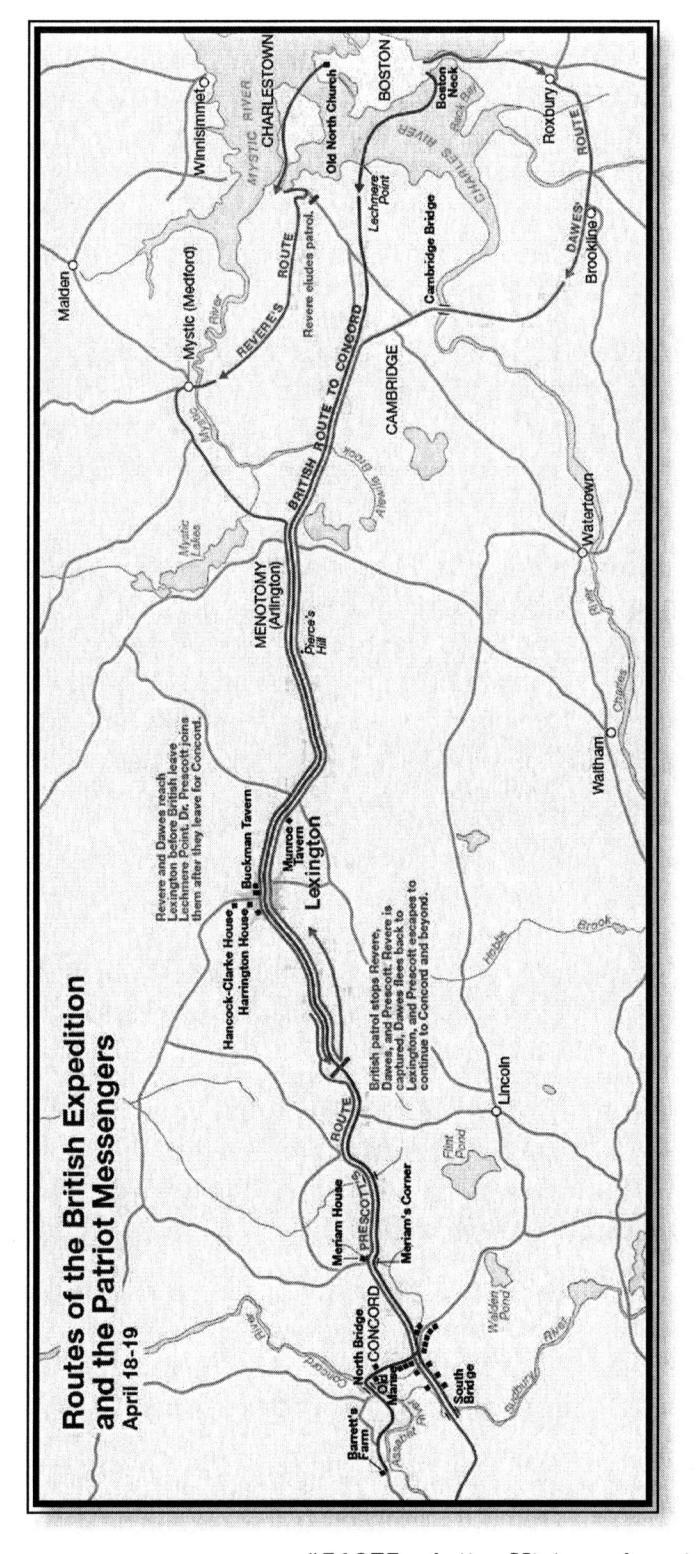

Battle Descriptions (cont.)

New York Campaign, 1776

In the last week of June in 1776, the British brothers Howe—General William Howe and Admiral Richard Howe—in a combined fleet and army of 35,000 men landed on Staten Island. They planned to attack and capture New York, and in the process destroy the American army under George Washington's command. New York was a Loyalist stronghold. By taking the city and moving up the Hudson River, the British had high hopes that they could cut off the troublesome New England settlements from the rest of the colonies. General Washington, anticipating General Howe's attack, moved his army to Long Island and made his headquarters in the fortifications on Brooklyn Heights on August 22, 1776. On this day, General Howe began to ferry his troops from Staten Island over to the Long Island shore.

General Howe moved swiftly. He had 22,000 soldiers to Washington's 10,000. Many of the American soldiers were new recruits and raw militia, and they broke and ran as they saw the British advance with glistening bayonets. On August 27, 1776, Washington's army was outsmarted, badly beaten, and forced to retreat. The American losses were 412 killed and 995 wounded. On the British side, 63 were killed and 275 were wounded.

After being badly beaten, the Americans scattered and fled into their fortifications at Brooklyn Heights. Washington knew his days were numbered. At night, Marblehead seamen from Rhode Island ferried Washington's troops over to Manhattan Island, escaping from the British. The entire American army slipped away. General Howe decided to attack New York instead of using his ships to land upriver and trap Washington. Again, the Americans slipped away and retreated to the northern end of Manhattan in late August, where they dug in and built forts and positions on Harlem Heights.

No explanation has ever been given as to why General Howe repeatedly allowed Washington and his army to slip out of his grasp. On September 16, 1776, the Battle of Harlem Heights was fought each side fielding (putting into action) about 5,000 soldiers. The Americans were yet to be formed into anything that roughly resembled an army. The British were professionals, but at Harlem Heights they received a bloody blow from the Americans. Washington's forces had 30 men killed and 90 wounded, while Howe lost 70 men and had 200 wounded.

The Americans managed to escape one more time in late October, moving up into what is called Westchester County today. A battle was fought at White Plains, and casualties were heavy on both sides. Washington was outnumbered two to one. The Americans lost 75 men, and 175 were wounded; Howe lost 40, and 200 were wounded.

General Howe's actions have never been satisfactorily explained. After the Battle of White Plains, Washington managed to move what remained of his army safely into New Jersey. The British were always right behind. General Howe could have used the British fleet to block Washington's escape, and yet again he committed a terrible mistake. Washington escaped with his army.

Battle Descriptions *(cont.)*

New York Campaign

Luxrunner

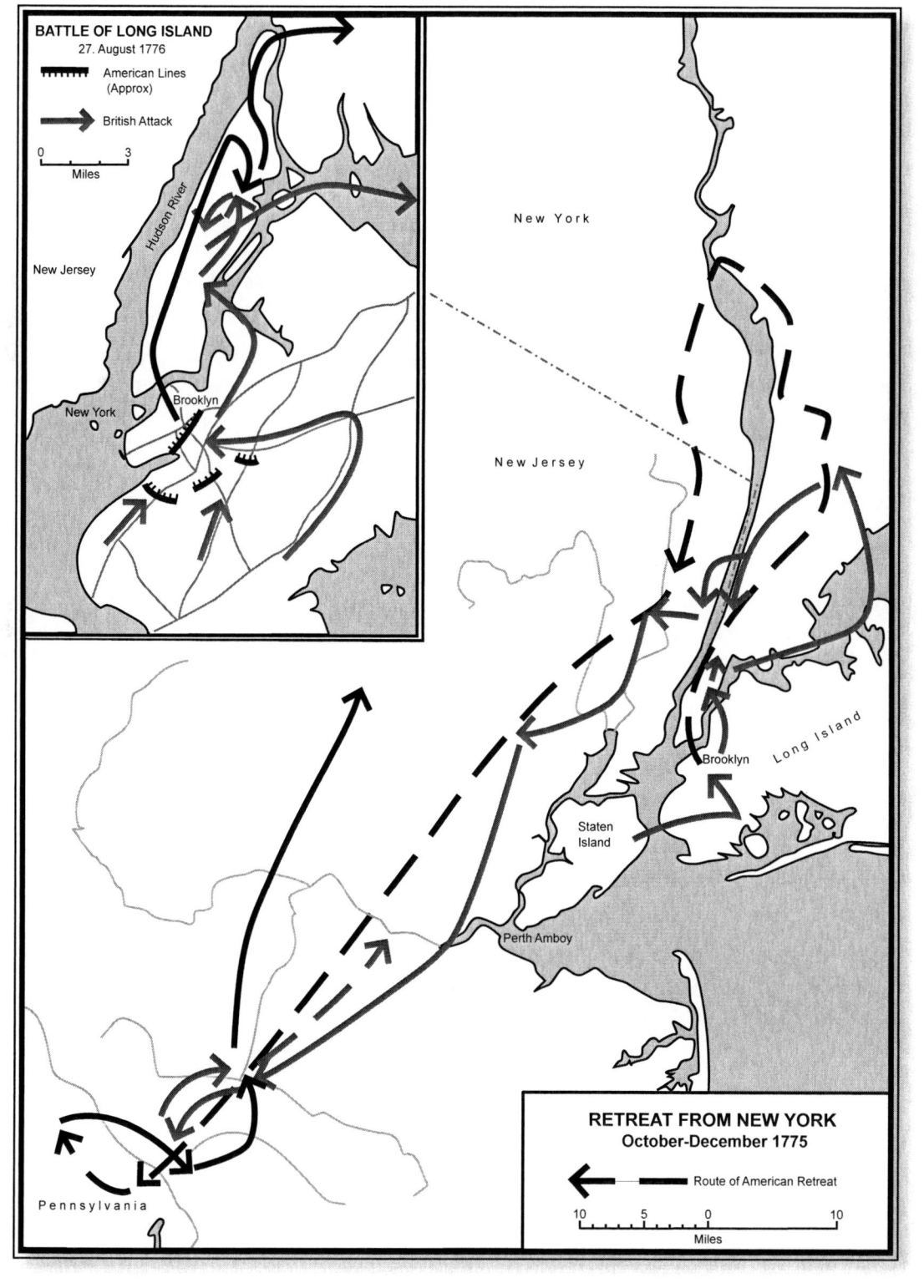

BATTLE OF LONG ISLAND
27. August 1776

American Lines (Approx)

British Attack

0   3
Miles

Hudson River

New Jersey

New York

Brooklyn

New York

New Jersey

Long Island

Brooklyn

Staten Island

Perth Amboy

Pennsylvania

RETREAT FROM NEW YORK
October-December 1775

Route of American Retreat

10   5   0   10
Miles

Battle Descriptions (cont.)

Battle of Trenton, 1776

The summer and fall of 1776 were disastrous for George Washington. As the leaves turned to red and gold, the Americans were in full retreat throughout New Jersey. The British were always close enough to be nipping at the heels of the defeated patriots, but Washington managed to stay just one step ahead. By November, it was looking worse. The American army was dwindling in numbers, and they were pushed across the Delaware River into Pennsylvania.

That November was the same month that the British went into winter quarters. The British were smug and satisfied with the campaign. As far as they were concerned, the revolution was finished. General Howe declared that no army ever stayed in the field and fought battles during the winter. The British were certain that Washington's troops would not have the ability, stamina, or courage to attack throughout the winter. With all of the confidence in the world, Manhattan and New York became a major British base. British soldiers held a scattering of outposts at Amboy, New Brunswick, Princeton, and Bordentown. The German troops under Howe's command were given the honor of guarding the Delaware Front, and they camped at Trenton.

On Christmas night of 1776, George Washington recrossed the ice-clogged Delaware River in the middle of a violent storm. (This is the subject of a famous painting that hangs in the rotunda of the nation's capitol "George Washington Crossing the Delaware," painted in 1851 by Emanuel Leutze.) The Americans trembled in the cold, for their uniforms were shredded rags. Blood in the snow left a trail where they marched, for many had broken boots and shoes, while others had bare feet wrapped in rags. The boats carrying soldiers, horses, and cannons were pushed by poles and rowed through massive chunks of ice by the same Marblehead seamen (from Marblehead, Massachusetts), whalers, and fishermen who rescued Washington's army after the Battle of Long Island.

Through the night, until the early hours of December 26 (midnight to 4:00 A.M.), the boats shuttled the American army back and forth across the Delaware River. A little after 4:00 A.M., Washington had his army assembled. They had a march of nine miles to reach Trenton. Muskets and powder were soaked from the storm, and Washington gave the command: "Tell General Sullivan to use the bayonet. I am resolved to take Trenton."

In the early morning light, at 7:30, Washington's troops attacked Trenton from several directions. Those Americans who had muskets and dried-out powder fired several rounds of gunfire, and other soldiers swept the enemy away with cannon fire. Trenton was a small-size town of some hundred-plus houses scattered about, and the fighting was the hottest in the streets. The German commanding officer moved angrily among his men, trying to rally his dazed soldiers. A blast of musket fire came from the American ranks, and the officer fell to the ground, mortally wounded.

The Americans rushed into the houses, and by 8:15 A.M., the Battle of Trenton was over almost as soon as it began. The attack had been a complete surprise, and the victory was total. The bulk of the German soldiers surrendered in an apple orchard. The Germans numbered 1,200. Of these, 36 were killed in the actual fighting, including their commanding officer, while 70 were listed as wounded. More than 1,000 of the Germans were taken prisoner, most of them bleary-eyed from an interrupted sleep and exhausted from the previous night's celebration of Christmas. Of the 2,400 soldiers under his command, Washington had four men killed and none wounded. At a time when it looked as if the revolution would die, George Washington gave Americans the hope that victory would come. The struggle would be long, and it would not be easy, but Americans would prevail.

Battle Descriptions (cont.)

Battle of Trenton

Center of Military History

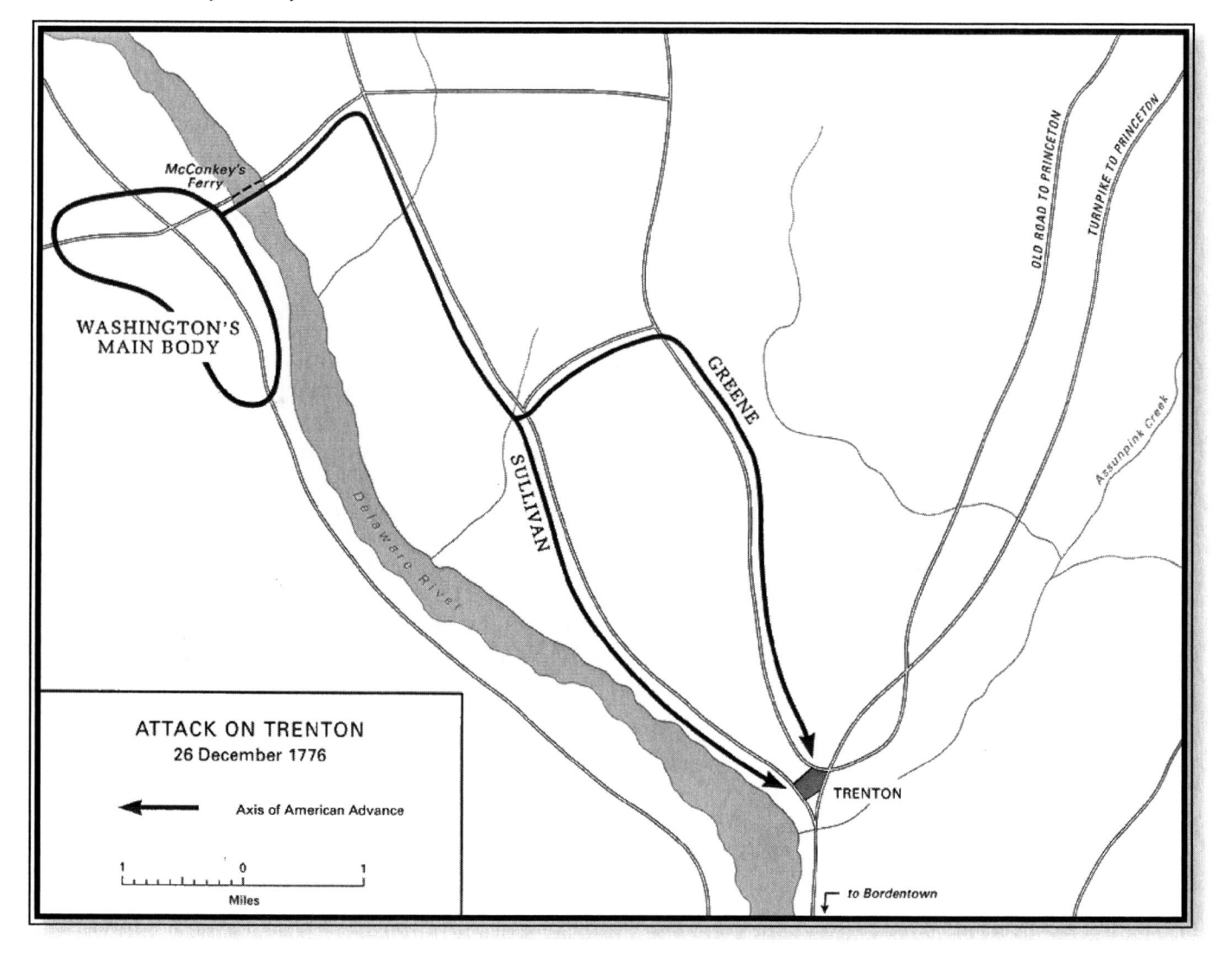

Battle Descriptions (cont.)

Battle of Saratoga, 1777

In the spring of 1777, the British designed a complicated plan to split New England from the other colonies. British General "Gentleman Johnny" Burgoyne was given command of an army that would drive down from Canada through Lake Champlain and Lake George on an invasion route. General Howe would move from New York with a fleet and an army up the Hudson River to join with General Burgoyne at Albany. This would drive a wedge between the middle colonies and the New England settlements. In the process, it would destroy George Washington's army if he dared to meet them in the open field.

After taking Fort Ticonderoga in early August, Burgoyne almost immediately began to run into trouble. Instead of using Lake George and the Hudson River to get his army to Albany, Gentleman Johnny chose to cut through the forest. Moving a few miles every day, hacking their way through the heavy undergrowth, his army became a tangled mess of artillery, baggage, troops, and camp followers. The woods were dense. The Americans, avoiding an open-pitched battle, cut down trees across their path at every opportunity in order to stop the British advance.

General Burgoyne made little progress. His army was running out of food and supplies, and the men were dropping from exhaustion and sickness. Burgoyne ordered a column of troops—1,000 men, mostly Germans and English Tories—across the border into the Hampshire Grants (Vermont today) to get food. At a small town called Bennington, the British were attacked and destroyed by American troops and militia under the command of General John Stark. Burgoyne lost more than 900 men in the encounter.

The American army, commanded by General Horatio Gates, grew stronger each day as militia swarmed into the area and swelled his ranks. On September 19, Burgoyne attacked the Americans at Freeman's Farm in Saratoga, but he was stopped in his tracks. The British still held out hope that they would be rescued. General Howe never received precise orders, so he took the initiative and struck at Philadelphia. General Clinton, in command at New York, sent a message to Burgoyne saying he hoped to push up the Hudson River with 2,000 men as reinforcements.

General Burgoyne launched a second attack at Freeman's Farm on October 7, which also resulted in heavy British losses. It was on this day at a critical moment in the battle that American General Benedict Arnold led a charge into the British positions, stopping the British advance and leaving the Americans holding the field. Arnold suffered a severe wound in his leg, which took him out of action for several months. The British losses in these two days of fighting were more than 1,200 men killed or wounded.

The army commanded by General John Burgoyne was completely surrounded. The British were outnumbered three to one, and more and more militia joined the American cause daily. Burgoyne's army had been shattered in the two engagements, his men were short of food and supplies, and so there was little left to do except ask for terms of surrender. On the 17th of October, General Burgoyne surrendered his army of 5,000 men to General Horatio Gates.

It was a great victory for the Americans. An entire British army that included professional German mercenaries had surrendered. Saratoga was a turning point in the war, for when the news reached Europe, the French agreed to a treaty of alliance with the United States. This assistance would enable the Americans to win the war.

Battle Descriptions (cont.)

Battle of Saratoga

Benson John Lossing

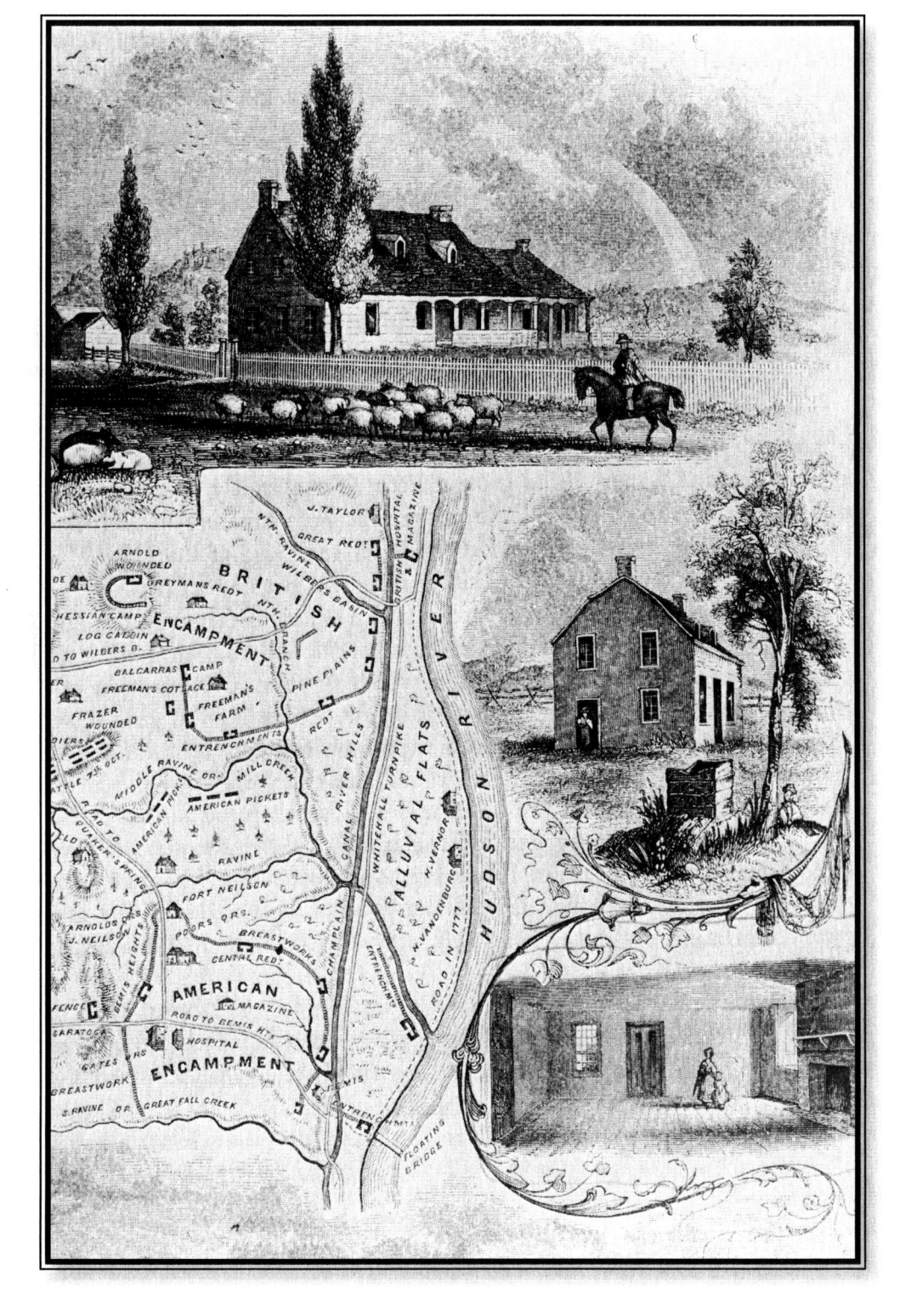

Battle Descriptions (cont.)

Battle of Yorktown, 1781

Following the disaster at Saratoga, the South became the battleground. General Cornwallis was given overall command of the British troops in the southern colonies. There was great expectation that large numbers of Southern Tories (American colonists loyal to King George III) would come running to help fight the rebels, but it simply did not work out that way. The British took Charleston and set up forts throughout the Carolinas, but the Americans continued to fight on stubbornly in spite of several severe defeats.

When George Washington and Congress placed General Nathaniel Greene in command of the American soldiers in the South, everything began to turn around. Throughout 1780 and 1781, the fighting was brutal. Francis Marion, called the "Swamp Fox," would hit the British whenever he could and then scurry and hide in the swamplands. At King's Mountain on October, 1780, Carolina backwoodsmen destroyed a force of 900 Southern Tories commanded by British officers. Cowpens, a battle fought on January 17, 1781, was a decisive victory for Greene and the Americans.

Two months later, in March, at Guilford Courthouse, British General Cornwallis paid a terrible price for a small victory and made the decision to move north into Virginia. Cornwallis joined Benedict Arnold, now wearing a British uniform and fighting for the king, and together they put Virginia to the torch. But the British were beginning to realize that they were not having any great success against the Americans. Furthermore, the Tories were not coming to help the British in any great numbers.

Cornwallis received orders to move his weary troops into Yorktown, Virginia, a little tobacco port on the York River. Here, the British dug in, built fortifications, and waited for the Royal Navy. His army would be evacuated. At the same time on August of 1781, American soldiers, under General LaFayette and General Von Steuben, moved into Virginia and were able to surround Cornwallis with his back to the sea.

General Washington's army, together with his French allies, was in the vicinity of New York when he received word that Cornwallis was trapped in Yorktown. The British in New York were led to believe that the French and Americans were preparing to attack. Instead, Washington moved all the troops speedily down into Virginia, where, on the 14th of September, he joined up with Lafayette. Over in Chesapeake Bay, a French fleet blocked the capes and, outmaneuvering the Royal Navy, prevented the evacuation of Cornwallis's army.

The American and French armies totaled 16,000 men. The British, caught behind their fortifications with nowhere to run, numbered 7,800. With Washington and his allies on all sides and with the French fleet blocking the Chesapeake, Cornwallis was in a hopeless position. On a daily basis, the British were battered by cannon fire. The French and Americans attacked repeatedly, probing the British defenses and getting closer. With each passing day, the British were running out of food and supplies. General Cornwallis knew that he would not get the help and the reinforcements he needed. He also realized that the Royal Navy would not come to his rescue.

On October 17, 1781, a defeated General Cornwallis surrendered his entire army to George Washington. As the British soldiers stacked their weapons and as the band played "The World Turned Upside Down," the prisoners marched off the battlefield in orderly ranks. Cornwallis lost 156 soldiers with 326 wounded, and the rest were worn and wearied by the long siege. The Americans and the French stood proudly at attention as the British marched through their ranks, and for the first time, the idea that independence was being won began to take hold.

Battle Descriptions *(cont.)*

Battle of Yorktown

S. G. Goodrich

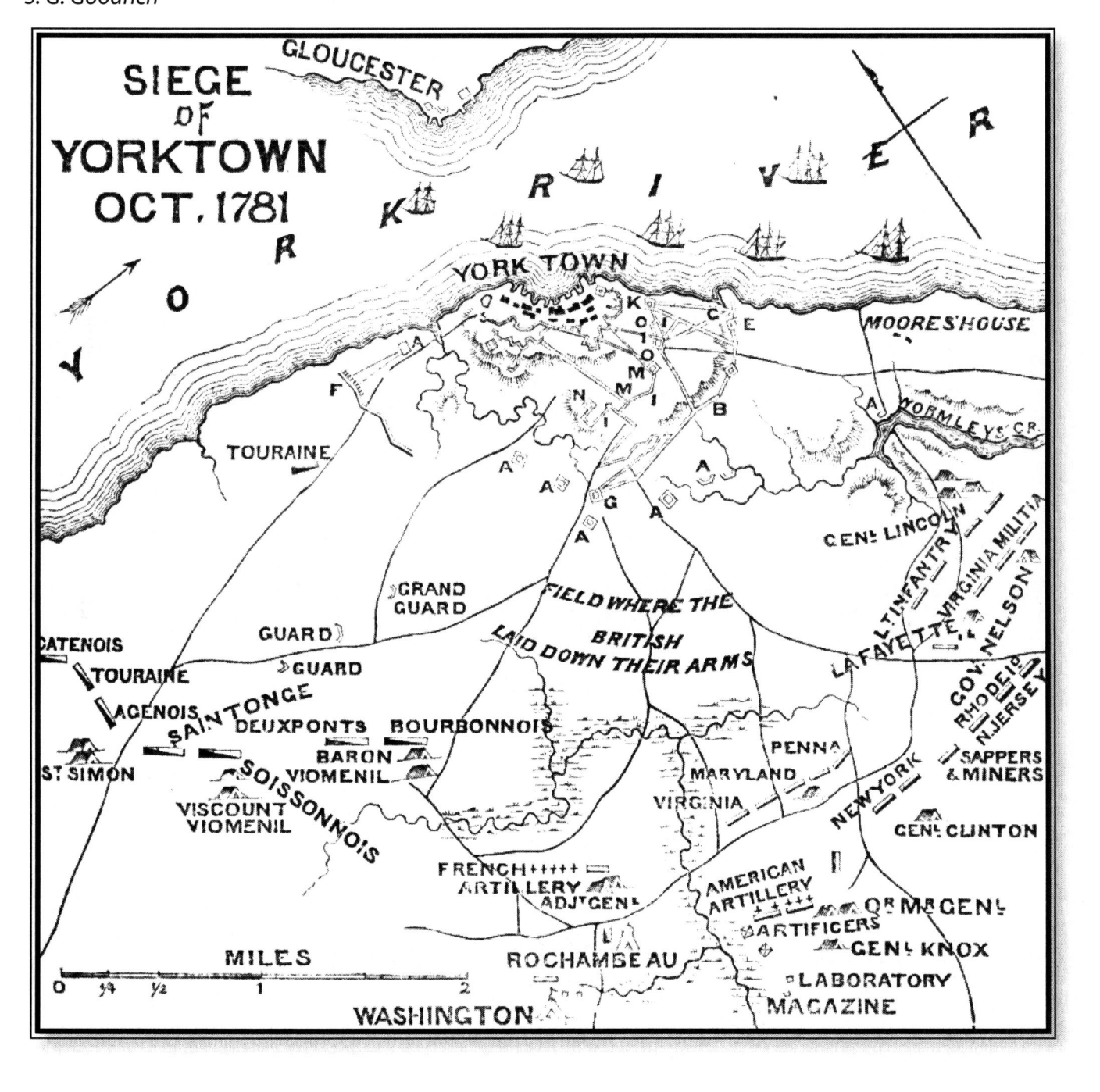

Steps for Making a Pocket Guide

1. Turn your paper horizontally. Fold the page into eight sections, as seen below. Using a pencil, lightly label each page, using the example below.

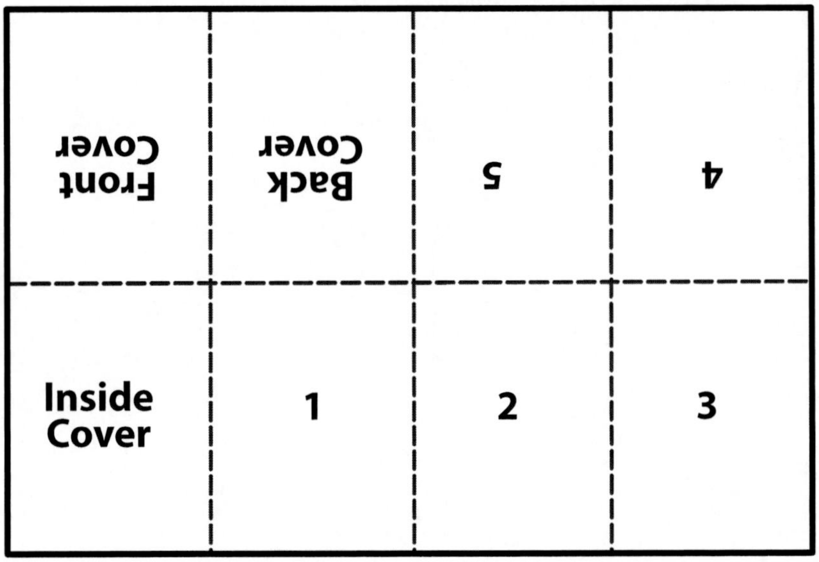

Front Cover
Back Cover
5
4
Inside Cover
1
2
3

2. Fold the middle into a tent and cut along the middle line, as seen in the example below. Do not cut all the way to the edge of the paper.

Inside Cover
2
3
4
5

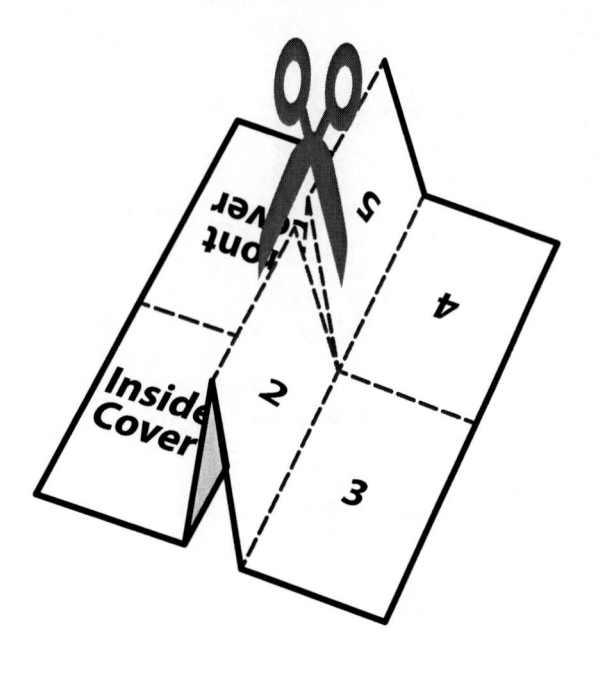

Steps for Making a Pocket Guide *(cont.)*

3. Pull the cut edge apart and down, as seen in the example below.

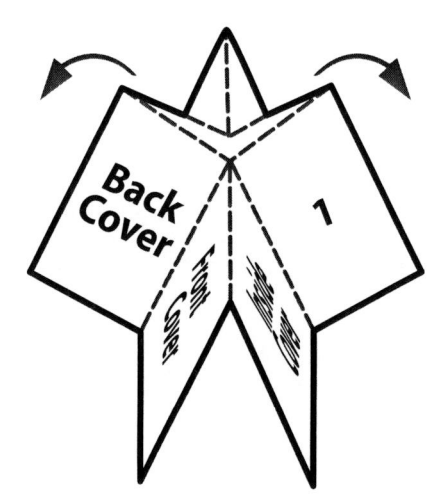

4. Fold the pages in the correct order.

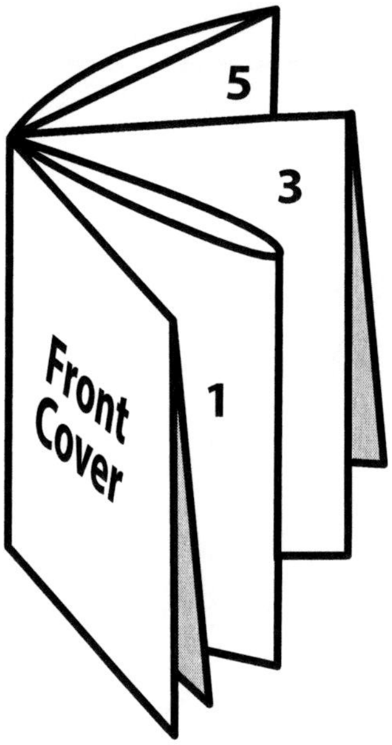

Name _____ Date _____

Organizing the Pocket Guide Information

Directions: Refer to the eight sections at the bottom of the page to storyboard your ideas for the pocket guide. The pages are numbered to show you how someone will read the pocket guide.

Front Cover—Place the title of your revolutionary battle on this page.

Inside Cover—Welcome the readers to the historical site. Give a brief overview of what they will discover (2–3 sentences) to get them excited about reading the pocket guide.

Page 1—Start with what happened before the battle. For example, what route did the troops use to get there, or for what reasons was that place chosen for the battle? Describe in detail what makes the place unique or special.

Page 2—Explain specifically how the battle began.

Page 3—Provide more details about the battle.

Page 4—Continue with details about the battle, showing a map of the place or some other visual to connect the reader.

Page 5—Describe specifically how the battle ended.

Back Cover—Thank the readers for "coming" to your tour. Add any other conclusion that is needed.

Front Cover	Back Cover	5	4
Inside Cover	1	2	3

Name _____ Date _____

Organizing the Audio Recording

Directions: Use this page to help you understand what needs to be included in your audio recording as well as what to write for the script.

Information

This recording is meant to complement the pocket guide. The things you talk about on the recording should go in the same order of the pocket guide. This audio recording should provide more details about the battle, and not simply be a reading of the script from the pocket guide.

Together we will negotiate criteria for assessment. Below are samples to consider:	
✓ The recording complements the pocket guide.	✓ The recording offers more information and details about the battle and people.
✓ The recording uses the same sequence/order as the pocket guide.	✓ The recording has sound effects.

Script Writing

You should have eight sections for your script. Follow the instructions below to write your script. Remember, be sure your audio has more detail and interesting facts than your pocket guide does.

Section 1—Place the title of your revolutionary battle on this page.

Section 2—Welcome the readers to the historical site. Give a brief overview of what they will discover (2–3 sentences) to get them excited about reading the pocket guide.

Section 3—Start with what happened before the battle. Examples might include how the troops got there or for what reason that place was chosen for the battle. Describe in detail what makes the place unique or special.

Section 4—Explain specifically how the battle began.

Section 5—Provide more details about the battle.

Section 6—Continue with details about the battle. Use a map of the place or some other visual to connect the reader.

Section 7—Describe specifically how the battle ended.

Section 8—Thank the readers for "coming" to your tour. Add any other conclusion that is needed.

Name _____ Date _____

Writing the Audio Script

Directions: Each section should last between 30 seconds and one minute. Write your script, using the lines below.

Section 1

_____

_____

_____

_____

_____

Section 2

_____

_____

_____

_____

_____

Section 3

_____

_____

_____

_____

_____

Name _____ **Date** _____

Writing the Audio Script *(cont.)*

Section 4

_____
_____
_____
_____
_____
_____
_____
_____

Section 5

_____
_____
_____
_____
_____
_____
_____
_____

Name _____ Date _____

Writing the Audio Script *(cont.)*

Section 6

_____

_____

_____

_____

_____

Section 7

_____

_____

_____

_____

_____

Section 8

_____

_____

_____

_____

_____

Name _____ Date _____

The Battles of the American Revolution

Directions: Use this chart to write down notes about the battles as you view the pocket guides and listen to the audio recordings.

Lexington and Concord	_____
New York Campaign	_____
Battle of Trenton	_____
Battle of Saratoga	_____
Battle of Yorktown	_____

Group Members' Names _____

_____ **Date** _____

American Revolution Assessment

Directions: Use the rubrics below to assess student work.

Pocket Guide Rubric

Criteria	1–2	3–4	5–6	7–8
Sections	Does not include all eight sections	Includes some sections	Includes most sections	Includes all sections
Battle Information	Does not focus on important battle information	Focuses on some important battle information	Focuses on most important battle information	Focuses on all important battle information in detail
Battle Overview	Does not include an overview of battle	Includes somewhat of an overview of battle	Includes an overview of battle	Includes a detailed overview of battle
Following Directions	Does not follow directions	Follows some of the directions	Follows most of the directions	Follows all of the directions
Layout and Design	No layout or design	Some layout and design	Adequate layout and design	Effective layout and design
Total Points: /40 pts.				

Audio Recording Rubric

Criteria	The recording complements the pocket guide	There are eight sections to the audio recording	The recording uses the same sequence/ order as the pocket guide	The recording offers more information and details about the battle	The recording has sound effects
None to Little					
Few to Some					
Good Amount					
Highly Detailed					

Forming a New Government

Objectives

- Students will analyze important measures that were attempted by the Confederation government by creating their own Articles of Confederation for a new government.
- Students will establish a set of laws describing what the new American nation needs.

Materials List

- Reproducibles (pages 106–112)

Overarching Essential Question

What is independence?

Standards

- McREL United States History Level III, 8.1
- CCSS.ELA-Literacy.CCRA.W.2
- CCSS.ELA-Literacy.CCRA.R.8

Guiding Questions

- In what ways did the articles reflect the values of the colonists?
- For what reasons do societies have laws?
- Describe in detail how the colonists created a more suitable government for themselves.
- For what reasons were the Articles of Confederation either successful or unsuccessful?

Suggested Schedule

The schedule below is based on a 45-minute period. If your school has block scheduling, please modify the schedule to meet your own needs.

Day 1	Day 2	Day 3	Day 4
Introductory Activity Students **write comic strips using the vocabulary** from this lesson in context.	Students are **assigned a grievance** and must **brainstorm a list** of ideas for **laws as solutions**.	Students **select the best idea** and **write an article** for the new Articles of Confederation and **compare it to the original**.	Students **evaluate** whether or not the government will survive based on a set of questions.

Forming a New Government *(cont.)*

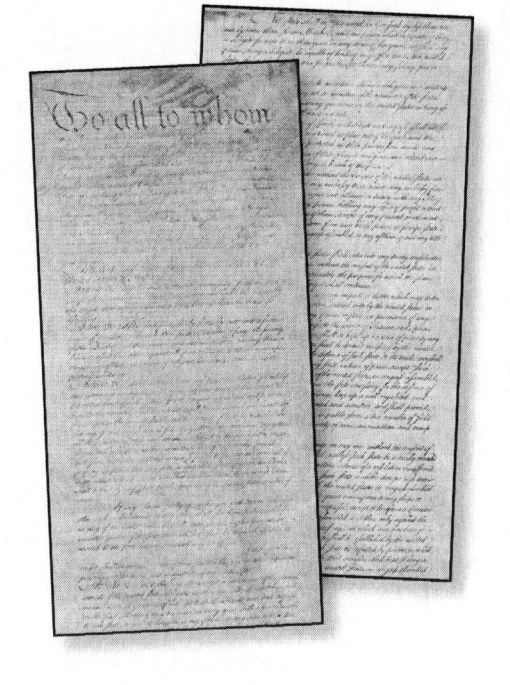

Day 1
Introductory Activity

1. To successfully complete this activity, students need to understand these essential terms:

   • grievance

   • article (section in a written document)

   • Articles of Confederation

2. Distribute copies of the *Comic Strip Vocabulary* sheet (page 106) to students. Have students create a comic strip using the terms listed above. Remind students to use the word in the context of the American Revolution time period.

3. Once students finish, have students share their comic strips with others sitting near them, checking to make sure they used the terms correctly. Allow a few students to share their comic strips with the entire class.

Note: Model the activity with students, guiding them through each step, as this may be unfamiliar to them.

Day 2

1. Display *The Scenario* (page 107) using an interactive board or projector (or make copies of it and hang them around the room). Read this scenario to the class.

2. Place students with partners, or in groups of three, and distribute copies of *American List of Grievances Against the King* (page 108). Students will use the vocabulary they learned from the previous day to help them understand this page. Read through this page aloud as if they were in a public forum or square and were reading the grievances to a crowd of people. The crowd can hold up their fingers: 1 for *somewhat agree*, 2 for *agree*, and 3 for *strongly agree* with the grievance.

3. Tell students that they are going to write articles for their new set of laws. Remind students that an *article* is a section in a written document. Explain that they will use the assigned grievance listed on this handout as a guide for the laws that they want. Assign a different grievance to each set of partners.

Forming a New Government (cont.)

4. Distribute copies of the *Brainstorming Ideas for Laws* sheet (page 109). Have students use the boxes on this page to brainstorm ideas for laws based on the grievances. Each idea should be written in a different box.

5. Have students set this page aside until the next day.

Day 3

1. Have students review their brainstormed list from the day before on the *Brainstorming Ideas for Laws* sheet (page 109). They can add to this list if desired.

2. Have students cut apart these ideas and place them in categories of *Good, Better*, and *Best* on their activity sheets. Students should select only one or two ideas from their lists to be placed in the *Best* category. Explain that they will use their best ideas in their new article, which will be part of the set of laws.

3. Distribute copies of the *Writing Your Article* sheet (page 110). Each group will write its portion of the Articles of Confederation based upon the grievances they have been assigned to rectify. Be sure to remind students that the people do not want a strong central government. They desire that the states retain powers so that a ruler like King George III will not threaten them again.

4. The class should then post their articles on the walls around the room so that everyone can read them. Give students a few minutes to view others' articles.

5. Distribute copies of the *Comparing the Class Articles to the Original Draft* (page 111) sheet and read it through as a class. Allow students to get up to once again to view the student-generated articles as they work to complete this page. The students will mark checks on the right side of the sheet if the items the class generated are included in the original draft. If students included any of these on their drafts, they are to mark an *X* on the right side of the sheet.

Day 4

1. Distribute the *Will the Government Survive?* sheet (page 112). There are two columns, one for the Articles of Confederation and one for the class articles. Students will determine whether the government will live or die, using what they have learned about the Articles of Confederation and their own generated articles.

2. Discuss student answers and how the two articles fared with these questions.

3. Have students form small groups to discuss the guiding questions in relation to this lesson.

Name _____ Date _____

Comic Strip Vocabulary

Directions: Use each of the vocabulary words in the comic strips below. Be sure to use it in the context of the American Revolution time period.

Vocabulary Word: Grievance

Vocabulary Word: Article (as in a section of a written document)

Vocabulary Word: Articles of Confederation

The Scenario

You are a colonist and are in the midst of fighting in the American Revolution against the British. You know that if the Americans cannot prove that they can govern themselves, you could fall right back under the rule of Great Britain. You have just signed the Declaration of Independence. Now, you need to establish a set of laws. What laws does your new nation need? First, you have to look at the problems to decide what kinds of solutions you need. In the Declaration of Independence, Thomas Jefferson made a list of grievances against King George III. Use these grievances to help you write the kinds of laws your nation will need.

The Scenario

You are a colonist and are in the midst of fighting in the American Revolution against the British. You know that if the Americans cannot prove that they can govern themselves, you could fall right back under the rule of Great Britain. You have just signed the Declaration of Independence. Now, you need to establish a set of laws. What laws does your new nation need? First, you have to look at the problems to decide what kinds of solutions you need. In the Declaration of Independence, Thomas Jefferson made a list of grievances against King George III. Use these grievances to help you write the kinds of laws your nation will need.

Name _____ Date _____

American List of Grievances Against the King

Directions: Your teacher will assign you one of the grievances below. Please circle it.

The king has taken the following actions:

1. Claimed to be above the law because of divine right (the belief that the king's rule comes directly from God, placing him above any human law)

2. Opposed needed laws

3. Neglected pressing problems

4. Demanded people give up their self-government before he approved needed laws

5. Made self-government inconvenient (no town meetings unless an agenda is submitted ahead of time)

6. Ordered lawmaking bodies to stop legislative meetings

7. Left the colonies unprotected after dissolving their legislatures

8. Tried to limit the growth and the expansion of the colonies

9. Interfered with justice in the colonies

10. Kept colonial judges under British control

11. Sent officers to harass the public

12. Quartered British soldiers in colonial homes without consent

13. Replaced civilian rule and law with martial law

14. Protected criminals

15. Limited trade

16. Taxed without consent

17. Denied trial by jury

18. Forced trials to be held overseas in England

19. Extended British rule into lands claimed by colonies

20. Changed colonial governments by taking away charters

21. Denied lawmaking powers

22. Destroyed lands and people

23. Hired mercenaries to fight Americans

24. Used Native Americans as allies against the colonists

25. Ignored peaceful offers and petitions of his subjects

Name _____ Date _____

Brainstorming Ideas for Laws

Directions: Follow the steps below to help you write your new article for a set of laws.

Write your grievance here: _____

_____

Brainstorm ideas for your laws based on your grievance above. Write one idea in each box. Use extra paper if needed.

Cut out the brainstormed ideas and place them in the appropriate columns below.

Good	Better	Best

Name _____ Date _____

Writing Your Article

Directions: You will use the grievance as a guide to write your new article, which will be part of the law of the land. Remember, as colonists, you do not want a strong government led by one leader. You want states to have more power. In the space below, write your article. An example is listed below.

Example

Grievance: The king must approve all imports and exports.

Article: All citizens can import and export as desired without any approval from the government.

New Article: _____

_____

_____

_____

_____

_____

_____

_____

_____

_____

_____

_____

_____

_____

_____

_____

_____

Name _____ **Date** _____

Comparing the Class Articles to the Original Draft

Directions: Under the Articles of Confederation, approved in November 1777, the Second Continental Congress had the impossible task of governing and protecting the states without a way to collect taxes or raise an army. At the same time, the states were writing their own constitutions. The Second Continental Congress worked out a plan to unify the states. This union is called a *confederation*. This confederation allowed many of the small governments to work toward a goal shared by all.

A. Add an *X* next to those items that match your list.

The Confederation Congress had the following powers:

   1. Pass laws with the consent of nine states _____

   2. Issue and borrow money _____

   3. Establish weights and measures _____

   4. Establish a postal service _____

   5. Declare war and make peace _____

   6. Establish an army and a navy _____

   7. Handle diplomatic affairs _____

B. Add an *X* next to those items that match your list.

The Confederation Congress did not have the following powers:

   1. Enforce its own laws _____

   2. Collect taxes or duties _____

   3. Control trade between the states _____

   4. Establish national courts to hear disputes between the states _____

C. Predict how well you think this government performed. Be sure to give reasons for your prediction.

   _____

   _____

   _____

Name _____ Date _____

Will the Government Survive?

Directions: Use what you now have learned about the Articles of Confederation to complete this page. Read each question below and check off whether or not the government would be able to handle each situation.

Questions	Articles of Confederation		Class Articles	
	Yes	No	Yes	No
1. The government wants to build an army. Can it demand money from the states?				
2. The Congress makes a deal with some of the native people of North America. Can it make this agreement?				
3. Two states are fighting over whether or not people should be allowed to carry goods between their borders. They are fighting over who should collect the taxes on the goods. Can this problem be settled by the central government?				
4. The government is facing a problem with Spain. It wants to send a representative overseas to straighten out the situation. Do the states have to provide the necessary money for ambassadors and diplomats (people who represent a country)?				
5. The government wants to place taxes on the large amounts of wine coming into the country from France as a way of collecting money. Is the government allowed to do so?				

Exercising Your Rights

Objectives

- Students will identify a political conflict at the state or local level after studying the foundations of American democracy.
- Students will research the issues involved in the conflict and examine the viewpoints on those issues.
- Students will exercise their democratic right and responsibility to actively participate in government by taking a stance, creating a political ad, and engaging in public debate about the issues.

Standards

- McREL Civics Level III, 28.1
- CCSS.ELA-Litearacy.CCRA.R.10
- CCSS.ELA-Litearcy.CCRA.W.8

Materials List

- Reproducibles (pages 118–128)
- Local newspapers (at least one week's worth)
- Democracy in America photographs

Overarching Essential Question

What is independence?

★ ★ ★

Guiding Question

- In what ways does democracy allow for emerging groups to become independent and recognized?
- Describe in detail how political campaigning brings multiple viewpoints to the surface.
- In what ways does democracy allow government to reflect the majority of its inhabitants' views?

Suggested Schedule

The schedule below is based on a 45-minute period. If your school has block scheduling, please modify the schedule to meet your own needs.

Day 1	Day 2	Day 3	Day 4	Day 5	Day 6
Students **identify political conflicts** that impact local residents.	Students **form a research plan** and begin to **look at two sides** of the issue.	Students **evaluate subjective** and **objective information** to aid them in their research.	Students **plan to make political ads** showing their position on their topic.	Students **finish their political ads** and **prepare to present** them the following day.	Students **present their political ads** to the class and **follow up with a debate/discussion** about these ads.

Exercising Your Rights *(cont.)*

Day 1

1. Ahead of time, collect at least one week's worth of current, local newspapers (both community newspapers and newspapers from the closest metropolitan region).

2. Remind students that conflict was present in all these lessons. First, the British Acts gave the reason for conflict between the colonists and the British. Second, the Mystery Boxes showed the individuals who were involved in the conflict. Third, the battles showed the physical conflict between the colonists and the British. Finally, the formation of the new government was based on the conflict. Explain that there is conflict all around us.

3. Ask students to browse through the newspapers in search of stories about political conflicts that impact local residents. Some examples include school district referendums; park district or forest preserve referendums; changes to city, county, or state laws; permits for new businesses or buildings; environmental issues, and immigration issues. Have students use the *Tracking Local Issues* sheet (page 118) to record what they find in the newspapers.

4. Replicate the *Tracking Local Issues* chart on the board or on chart paper. Record students' findings on the class chart. At this time, answer students' questions about the issues. Clarify details and correct misinformation if necessary.

5. Distribute the *So What?* sheet (page 119) to students. Complete one of the network trees together as a whole class. Have students complete the rest independently.

6. Place students in small groups for a discussion about the *So What?* sheet. Ask them to talk about the ways political conflicts impact their lives.

7. Prior to teaching this lesson, write in the issues or political conflicts that students identified in the previous activity on the *Ranking the Issues* ballots (page 120). Make copies and distribute them to students. Have students rank the three political conflicts that interest them the most.

★ ★ ★

Exercising Your Rights *(cont.)*

Day 2

1. Remind students that participation in government at any level is a right and a responsibility. The Founding Fathers fought the American Revolution to secure this right for us. Explain to students that they will have an opportunity to engage in America's democracy.

2. Place students in small groups (project teams) based on their secret-ballot rankings. Make sure that each student has one of his or her top three topic choices. Personal choice is essential in motivating students to civic engagement.

3. Distribute the *Getting Started* sheet (page 121) to students. Project teams should work together to formulate a research plan. Circulate and assist as needed.

4. Distribute the *Take Action* sheet (page 122). Action steps should include background research, daily monitoring of traditional and nontraditional news sources, and interviews with a variety of people. Provide time in and out of class for students to complete their action steps.

5. Distribute the *Two Views* sheet (page 123) to each student. As they learn more about the political conflict, they should be able to clearly define the two (or more) sides of the issue.

Day 3

1. As students conduct their research, they will encounter a variety of sources, some objective and some subjective.

2. Review the meanings of objectivity and subjectivity using the *Objective or Subjective?* sheets (pages 124–125). Place students with partners.

3. Distribute the *Objective or Subjective?* sheets (pages 124–125) to each pair of students. Provide a variety of newspapers, magazines, online news sources, fliers, and brochures from which students can choose two pieces of information to evaluate.

4. Wrap up the objective and subjective mini lesson with a class discussion about students' findings. Remind students to consider the objectivity or subjectivity of their sources as they research their topics.

Exercising Your Rights *(cont.)*

Day 4

1. Display the images included on the Digital Resource CD of Americans participating in democracy.

   • A 1912 photo shows suffragettes holding a parade for women's voting rights.

   • A 1938 photo shows a U.S. representative reading telegraphs that were sent to protest a bill.

   • A 1965 photo shows a group of participants marching from Selma to Montgomery, Alabama during the civil rights movement.

   • A 2008 photo shows delegates with signs at the Democratic National Convention.

2. Have students brainstorm all the different ways people participate in having their voices heard. Tell students that there are many different ways to participate in having their voices heard, such as marching in parades, writing letters, and attending political events. Explain that just because young people cannot vote does not mean that they cannot participate in government.

3. Students have researched the political conflict in depth and examined both sides of the issue. They are now ready to declare their support for one side in the political conflict. Distribute the *Take a Stand: Political Ads Graphic Organizer* sheet (page 126) to students. Students will use this page to organize their viewpoints, evidence, and solutions. Prior to filling out the graphic organizer, model the three different formats for students. They should generate a list of what makes the ad strong. Have students compare and contrast two different ones, a weak one and a stronge one, so that they get the sense of what is needed for that format. Then before designing anything, negotiate the criteria for assessment with students.

4. Give students time to fill out this page and organize their ideas. At this point, it is time to embark on the negotiable contracting of assessment with students. If they were the teacher, what criteria would they be looking at in order to assess their project? What makes quality work?

5. Distribute copies of the *Political Ads Checklist* sheet (page 127) so students know how their work will be evaluated.

6. Students should begin working on their editorials, commercials, and print advertisements for homework.

Exercising Your Rights *(cont.)*

Day 5

1. Give students class time to finish their editorials, commercials, and print advertisements.

2. Provide help as needed. Remind students to look at the checklist to make sure they have all the elements as discussed in the negotiable contracting process.

3. Explain that they will be delivering their final political ad to the class the following day.

Day 6

1. Have students present their editorials, commercials, and print advertisements to the class. Use the *Political Ads Assessment* sheet (page 128) to assess student work as a guide or you could draft your own with students. At this point, embark on the negotiable contracting process, making sure that the students know the criteria that will make their guide outstanding. A rubric can be designed for students using the criteria of assessment.

2. Require students to comment on one another's positions. Set parameters for civil debate on issues. This will prepare students to engage effectively and appropriately in the public debate.

3. Students will engage in the public debate about their topics. Students could comment on online newspaper articles, express their views on blogs or websites, write letters to newspaper editors, make posters, distribute fliers, attend public meetings, set up information booths, join political groups, or participate in and/or organize special events.

4. Have students engage in a discussion about the essential question *What is conflict?*

Name _____ Date _____

Tracking Local Issues

Directions: Browse at least one week's worth of local newspapers. Identify current conflicts that impact you and others in your community. Record your findings on the chart below.

Description of Issue	Viewpoint 1	Viewpoint 2	Other Details	Key Dates

Name _____ **Date** _____

So What?

Directions: For what reasons should you care about the political conflicts in your community? Complete the graphic organizer below to find out why these issues matter to you.

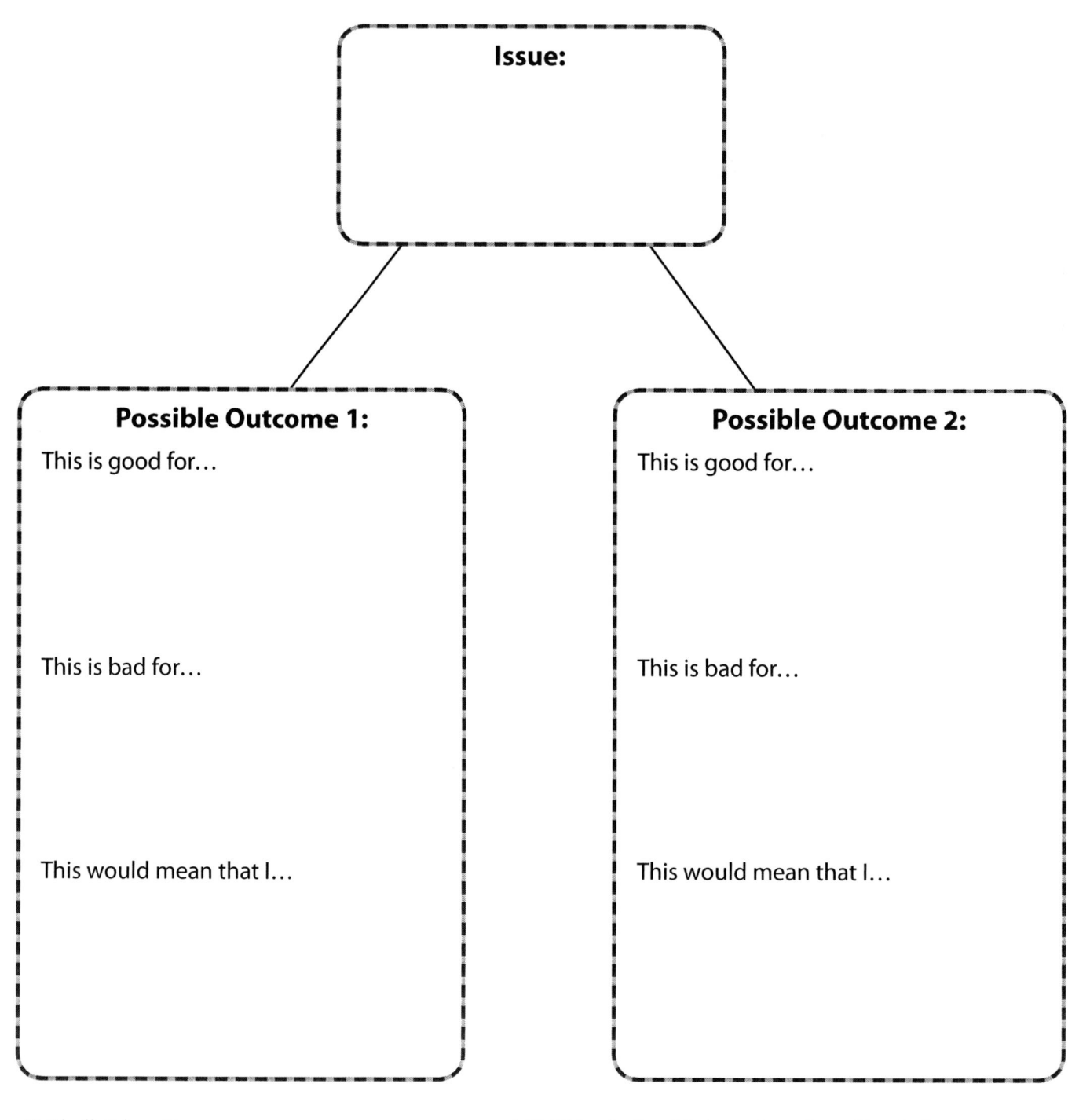

Name _____ Date _____

Ranking the Issues

Secret Ballot

Directions: This secret ballot will determine the topic of your final project. Place a number 1 on the line next to your first choice for a topic, a number 2 by your second choice, and a number 3 by your third choice.

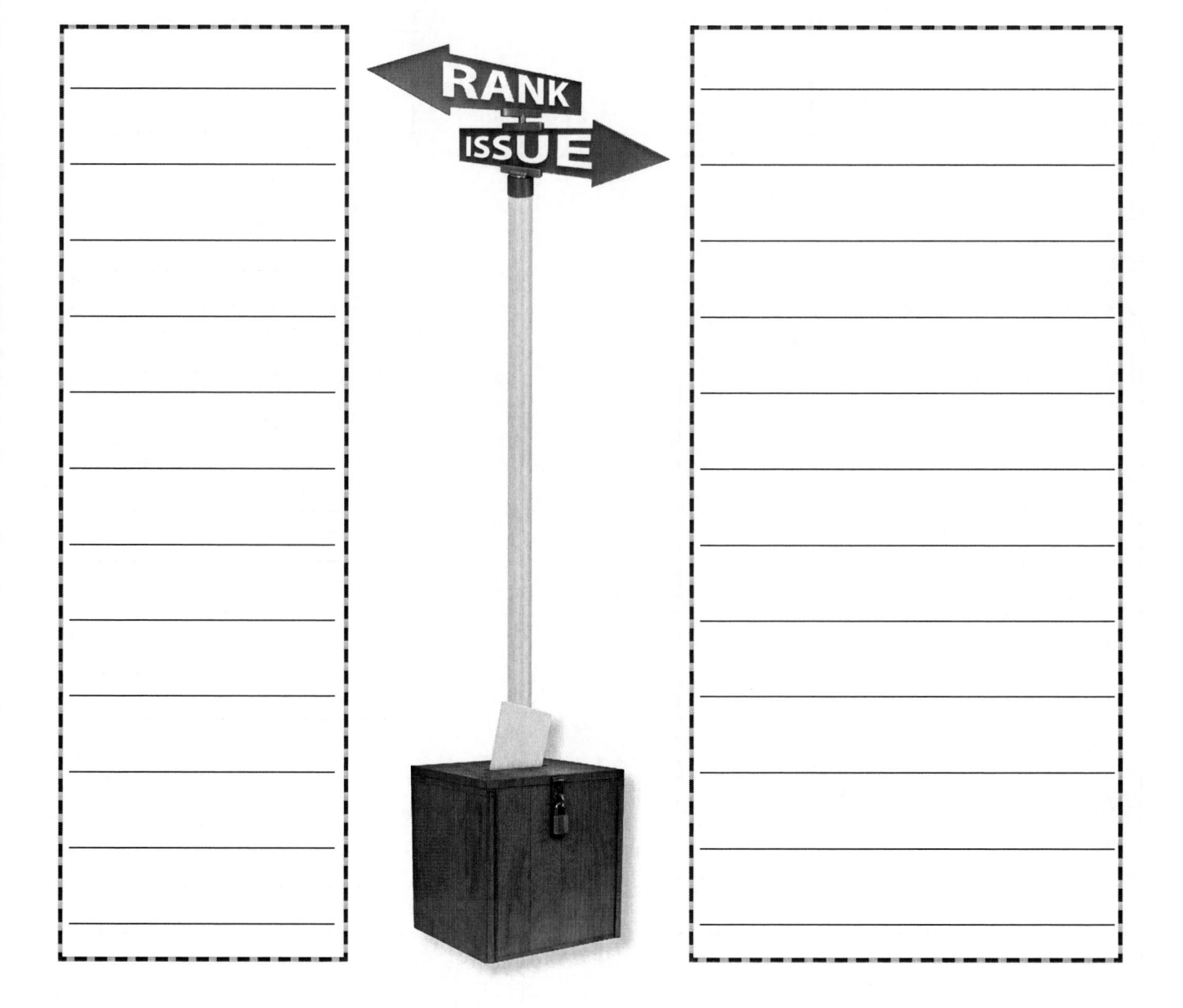

Name _____ **Date** _____

Getting Started

Directions: Work with your project team to complete the research plan below.

1. **Conflict summary:** _____
   _____
   _____
   _____

2. **Viewpoint 1 contacts** (names of people and groups, addresses of relevant websites, meeting dates and locations, etc.)**:** _____
   _____
   _____
   _____

3. **Viewpoint 2 contacts** (names of people and groups, addresses of relevant websites, meeting dates and locations, etc.)**:** _____
   _____
   _____
   _____

4. **Traditional news sources** (newspapers, television, radio)**:** _____
   _____

5. **Non-traditional news sources** (blogs, social media, fliers, etc.)**:** _____
   _____

6. **Sources of background information:** _____
   _____
   _____

Name _____ **Date** _____

Take Action

Directions: Work together with your group to identify action steps for each project team member. Complete the chart below with the person's name, action to take, due date, and purpose.

Student Name	Will . . . (action to take)	By . . . (due date)	To find out . . . (purpose)

Name _____ **Date** _____

Two Views

Directions: Complete the chart to define the two (or more) sides of the conflict. For each viewpoint, identify *Who* is on that side of the conflict, *What* they want, *Why* they want it, and *How* they plan to get it.

Viewpoint:	Viewpoint:
Who?	
What?	
Why?	
How?	

Name _____ Date _____

Objective or Subjective?

Directions: Find examples of objective information and examples of subjective information in newspapers, magazines, online news sources, and fliers. Use the chart and questions below to verify each publication's objectivity or subjectivity.

Objective Information	Subjective Information
• Factual • Can be observed, measured, or counted • Unbiased (neutral in opinion) • Free of personal feelings and opinions • Contains facts that can be checked • Often presents multiple points of view	• Is based on personal feelings • Expresses opinions • Is biased and presents one point of view • Lacks observable, measurable evidence • May rely on fear tactics or extreme language to convey the message

Title/Author: _____

Publication: _____

1. Describe in detail the author's political position. _____

2. In what other ways does the publication of the information affect the author? _____

   _____

3. Was the information published for free (as in a news story), or did someone pay to have it published (as in a direct mail flier)? If someone paid for the message, who was it? _____

   _____

4. Describe in detail the tone, or feeling, of the piece._____

   _____

5. Does the author cite sources or statistics? If so, find out more about the data. _____

   _____

6. After answering the questions above, please explain specifically if the piece is objective or subjective. Explain. _____

   _____

Name _____ **Date** _____

Objective or Subjective? *(cont.)*

Title/Author: _____

Publication: _____

1. Describe in detail the author's political position. _____

2. In what other ways does the publication of the information affect the author? _____
    _____

3. Was the information published for free (as in a news story), or did someone pay to have it
    published (as in a direct mail flier)? If someone paid for the message, who was it? _____
    _____

4. Describe in detail the tone, or feeling, of the piece. _____
    _____

5. Does the author cite sources or statistics? If so, find out more about the data. _____
    _____
    _____
    _____

6. After answering the questions above, please explain specifically if the piece is objective or
    subjective. Explain your answer in detail. _____
    _____
    _____
    _____
    _____

Name _____ Date _____

Take a Stand: Political Ads Graphic Organizer

The purpose of a political ad is not just to promote a candidate. It can also be used is to generate support for a particular point of view on an issue. Your political ad should describe a stance, or position, on the issue and provide a rationale (explanation) for that view.

Select one of the following formats:

- Commercial (shorter than one minute)
- Print advertisement (such as a poster)
- Editorial for a local newspaper

Directions: Use the graphic organizer to plan the elements needed in your political ad.

Issue:		
Your Position:		
Reason 1	**Supporting Evidence**	**Supporting Evidence**
Reason 2	**Supporting Evidence**	**Supporting Evidence**
Reason 3	**Supporting Evidence**	**Supporting Evidence**
Solution	**Suggested Action**	

Name _____ Date _____

Political Ads Checklist

Directions: As you create your political ad, be sure your ad includes the following items:

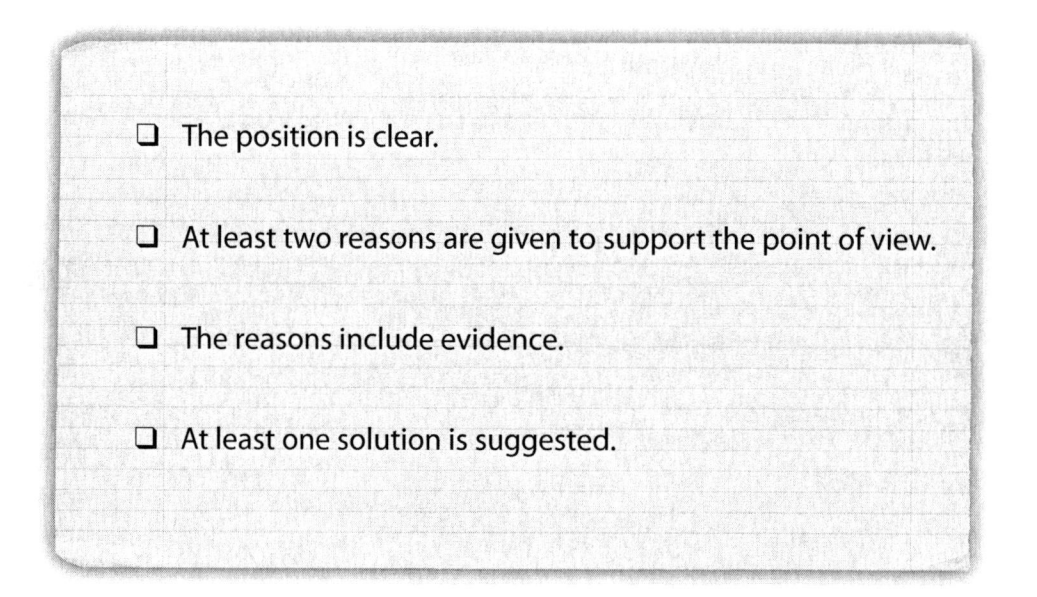

❑ The position is clear.

❑ At least two reasons are given to support the point of view.

❑ The reasons include evidence.

❑ At least one solution is suggested.

Political Ads Assessment

Directions: Use the point-based rubric to assess student political ads.

Criteria	Mayor (Level I)	Governor (Level II)	Congressman (Level III)	President (Level IV)	
Position	Political position is not clear (1–3 pts.)	Political position is somewhat clear (4–6 pts.)	Political position is clear (7–9 pts.)	Political position is clear and detailed (10–12 pts.)	/12 pts.
Reasoning and Support	No reasons are provided to support point of view (1–3 pts.)	Some reasoning are provided to support point of view (4–6 pts.)	Two reasons are provided to support point of view (7–9 pts.)	Two reasons and detailed descriptions are provided to support point of view (10–12 pts.)	/12 pts.
Evidence	Reasons do not include evidence (1–3 pts.)	Reasons include some evidence (4–6 pts.)	Reasons include evidence (7–9 pts.)	Reasons include detailed evidence (10–12 pts.)	/12 pts.
Solution	No solution is suggested (1–2 pts.)	Weak solution is suggested (3–4 pts.)	Adequate solution is suggested (5–6 pts.)	Detailed solution is suggested (7– 8 pts.)	/8 pts.
Comments:					**Total Points:** /44 pts.

References Cited

Conklin, Wendy, and Andi Stix. 2014. *Active Learning Across the Content Areas*. Huntington Beach, CA: Shell Education.

Crane, Thomas. 2002. *The Heart of Coaching: Using Transformation Coaching to Create a High-Performance Culture*. San Diego, CA: FTA Press.

Danielson, Charlotte. 2011. "The Framework for Teaching." The Danielson Group. http://www .danielsongroup.org/article.aspx?page=frameworkforteaching.

Jacobs, Heidi H. 2010. *Curriculum 21: Essential Education for a Changing World*. Alexandria, VA: Association for Supervision and Curriculum Development.

King, F. J., Ludwika Goodson, and Faranak Rohani. 1998. *Higher-Order Thinking Skills*. Tallahassee, FL: Center for Advancement of Learning and Assessment.

Kise, Jane A. G. 2006. *Differentiated Coaching: A Framework for Helping Teachers Change*. Thousand Oaks, CA: Corwin Press.

Latrhop, L., Vincent, C., and Annette M. Zehler. 1993. *Special Issues Analysis Center Focus Group Report: Active Learning Instructional Models for Limited English Proficient (LEP) Students*. Report to U.S. Department of Education, Office of Bilingual Education and Minority Languages Affairs (OBEMLA). Arlington, VA: Development Associates, Inc.

Michalko, Michael. 2006. *Thinkertoys: A Handbook of Creative-Thinking Techniques*. Berkeley, CA: Ten Speed Press.

National Council for the Social Studies. 2008. "A Vision of Powerful Teaching and Learning in the Social Studies: Building Social Understanding and Civic Efficacy." Position statement. http://www.ncss.org /positions/powerful.

Scriven, Michael, and Richard Paul. 1987. "Defining Critical Thinking." Dillion Beach, CA: National Council for Excellence in Critical Thinking Instruction. 1996. http://www.criticalthinking.org.

Stix, Andi. 2012. "Essential and Guiding Questions." *Stix Pix for the Interactive Classroom*. Accessed April 29. http://www.andistix.com/essential_and_guiding_questions.

Stix, Andi, and Frank Hrbek.1999. "A Rubric Bank for Teachers." *The Interactive Classroom*. Accessed on August 14. http://www.andistix.com.

———. 2006. *Teachers as Classroom Coaches*. Alexandria VA: Association for Supervision and Curriculum Development.

Zmuda, Allison. 2008. "Springing into Active Learning." *Educational Leadership* 66 (3): 38–42.

About the Authors

Andi Stix Ed.D., and PCC, is a national educational consultant, administrator, teacher, and certified life and instructional coach. In addition to teaching for over 35 years, Dr. Stix has been a presenter at seminars and a keynote speaker. Andi earned her doctorate in Gifted Education from Columbia University and currently owns and operates the Interactive Classroom, an education-consulting firm in New Rochelle, New York. Dr. Stix founded and runs the award-winning afterschool enrichment program for bright, curious, and clever-minded children, G·tec Kids. Through her work, Andi continues to be an advocate for Synergy Westchester where she focuses on the needs of teachers and families of gifted learners. Her articles have appeared in *Social Education*, *Middle School Journal*, *Social Studies*, *Arithmetic Teacher*, *The Math Notebook*, *ERIC*, and *Gems of AGATE*. Along with her co-author, Frank Hrbek, Andi has written *Teachers as Classroom Coaches*, which focuses on integrating coaching strategies into the fabric of the educational system. Together, they have also written the *Exploring History* series of simulations and hands-on investigations in history for the secondary school market. For her work in professional development, Andi received the Alexinia Baldwin Educator of the Year Award. Books Dr. Stix has authored include *Using Literature and Simulations in Your Social Studies Classroom, Integrated Cooperative Strategies for the Social Studies, Language Arts, and the Humanities*. For fun and useful activities, please refer to Andi Stix's blog at andistix.com.

Frank Hrbek, M.A., is the co-author of the *Exploring History* and *Active History* series. A well-established educator, Mr. Hrbek has spent the past 40 years teaching middle school social studies in New York City. He holds a Master of Arts in History after having received a degree in English, with minors in journalism and history, at New York University. Mr. Hrbek works alongside Dr. Stix, attending workshops, conferences, and presenting at colleges. He has successfully integrated many of Dr. Stix's new coaching and cooperative learning strategies in his own classroom. Their series, *Exploring History*, is a three-time winner of the New York State's Social Studies Program of Excellence Award, as well as Middle States Council for the Social Studies' Social Studies Program of Excellence Certificate. The series also received the Outstanding Curriculum Development Award from the National Association of Gifted Children, and is a two-time winner of the Teacher's Choice Award from Learning magazine.

Contents of Digital Resource CD

Reproducibles and Resources		
Page	**Activity Sheet**	**Filename/Folder Name**
24–27	Student Glossary	glossary.pdf
28-29	The Proclamation of 1763	proclamation.pdf
30–31	The Sugar Act	sugaract.pdf
32–33	The Colonial Currency Act	colonial.pdf
34–35	The Quartering Act	quartering.pdf
36–37	The Stamp Act	stamp.pdf
38–39	The Declaratory Act	declaratory.pdf
40–41	The Townshend Acts	townshend.pdf
42–43	The Tea Act	tea.pdf
44–45	The Quebec Act	quebec.pdf
46–47	The Intolerable Acts	intolerable.pdf
48	Skit Planning Sheet	skitplanning.pdf
49	Set the Scene	setscene.pdf
50	Storyboard the Skit	storyboardskit.pdf
51–53	Keeping Track of the Acts	keepingtrack.pdf
54	Skit Assessment	skitassessment.pdf skitassessment.doc
66	Creative Introductions	creative.pdf
67–69	Calling Cards from the American Revolution	callingcards.pdf
70	Inquiring Minds	inquiringminds.pdf
71	Primary Source Analysis	primary.pdf
72	Writing Introductions	writingintro.pdf
73	Introductions Rubric	introrubric.pdf introrubric.doc
74	How to Make a Mystery Box	box.pdf
75	Mystery Box Project Rubric	boxrubric.pdf boxrubric.doc
76	Mystery Box Game Chart	boxgamechart.pdf
82	American Revolution Conversations	americanconv.pdf

Contents of Digital Resource CD (cont.)

Reproducibles and Resources		
Page	**Activity Sheet**	**Filename/Folder Name**
84–93	Battle Descriptions	battledescr.pdf
94–95	Steps for Making a Pocket Guide	pocketguide.pdf
96	Organizing the Pocket Guide Information	pocketorganize.pdf
97	Organizing the Audio Recording	audioorganize.pdf
98–100	Writing the Audio Script	audiowrite.pdf
101	The Battles of the American Revolution	battles.pdf
102	American Revolution Assessment	americanassess.pdf americanassess.doc
106	Comic Strip Vocabulary	comicstrip.pdf
107	The Scenario	scenario.pdf
108	American List of Grievances Against the King	grievances.pdf
109	Brainstorming Ideas for Laws	brainstorming.pdf
110	Writing Your Article	writing.pdf
111	Comparing the Class Articles to the Original Draft	comparing.pdf
112	Will the Government Survive?	survive.pdf
118	Tracking Local Issues	tracking.pdf
119	So What?	sowhat.pdf
120	Ranking the Issues	ranking.pdf
121	Getting Started	started.pdf
122	Take Action	action.pdf
123	Two Views	views.pdf
124–125	Objective or Subjective?	objectivesub.pdf
126	Take a Stand: Political Ads Graphic Organizer	takeastand.pdf
127	Political Ads Checklist	politicalads.pdf
128	Political Ads Assessment	poladassess.pdf poladassess.doc

Contents of Digital Resource CD *(cont.)*

Teacher Resources	
Activity Sheet	**Filename/Folder Name**
Rubric Bank for Teachers	rubricbank.pdf rubricbank.doc
Democracy in America Photographs	demphotos.pdf
GOPER Model	gopermodel.pdf

Correlation Charts	
Correlation Charts	**Filename/Folder Name**
CCSS, WIDA, TESOL, McREL, and NCSS	standards.pdf

Notes

#51075—*Active History: American Revolution*

Notes

Notes